34 KING STREET, COVENT GARDEN, LONDON, W.C. 2

By A. R. Florian.

Grammar of Modern French. 3s. 6d.

Elementary French Grammar. 2s. 6d.

French Exercises. 3s.

French Prose Composition. 3s.

Elementary French Reading. 2s. 9d.

Preliminary French Course. 2s. 6d.

A First French Course. 3s. 6d.
The First Twenty-eight Lessons and their Special Vocabularies Phonetically Transcribed. 1s. 6d.

A Second French Course. 3s.

Passages for Translation into French. Junior, 1s. 6d. Senior, 2s.

French Unseens. Junior, 1s. 6d.

French Unseens. Senior, 2s.

French Test Papers. Junior and Senior, 1s. each.

French Grammatical Readers.

Series A. With Vocabularies. 2s. 6d. each.
Le Blocus, par ERCKMANN-CHATRIAN. L'Evasion d'Edmond Dantès, par DUMAS. L'Homme à l'Oreille Cassée, par ABOUT.

Series B. With or without Vocabularies, 2s. 6d. each.
Nouvelles Genevoises, par TÖPFFER. Le Capitaine Pamphile, par DUMAS. Contes Choisis.

French Unseens. By S. E. LONGLAND.
Junior—2 books. 8d. each.
Senior—2 books. 10d. each.

A French Grammar for higher classes.
By F. V. MASSARD and C. DURNO. 4s.

By F. V. Massard.

A French Exercise Book.
A companion volume to above. 3s.

Elementary French Composition—
Direct Method. 3s.

A French Composition Book—
Direct Method. 3s.

Direct Method French Readers.

Junior Series:—With Vocabularies. 2s. 6d. each. La Mare au Diable, par G. SAND. Quatre Contes, par MÉRIMÉE. Lettres de mon Moulin, par DAUDET. Deux Nouvelles: Pierre et Camille, et Croisilles, par ALFRED DE MUSSET.

Senior Series:—No Vocabularies. 3s. each. Bug-Jargal, par HUGO. Pêcheur d'Islande, par LOTI. Colomba, par MÉRIMÉE. Le Roi des Montagnes, par EDMOND ABOUT.

By A. R. Florian.

First Book of German Oral Teaching on the Direct Method. 4s. 6d.

German Unseens. 3s. 6d.

German Test Papers. Junior and Senior. 1s. each.

A Primer of German Grammar.
By SOMERVILLE and BYRNE. 3s.

A First German Writer.
By the same Authors. 4s.

German Prose Composition.
By R. J. MORICH. 5s.

Deutsches Exerzieren. Compiled and Edited by S. TINDALL. 5s.

Das Deutsche Zeitwort in Bewegung. By S. TINDALL. 2s.

A Practical German Course.
By S. TINDALL. 3s. 6d.

Deutsche Märchen und Sagen (being a first German Reading Book). By S. TINDALL. 2s. 6d.

A German Composition Book.
By F. V. MASSARD. 3s. 6d.

An Introductory History of English Literature. With Illustrative Passages. By G. A. TWENTYMAN.
Vol. I. Early Times to the Elizabethan Age. 6s.
Vol. II. The Seventeenth Century to the Romantic Period. 6s.
Vol. III. The Victorian Age and the Literature of America. 6s.
The HISTORY only, without the Illustrative Passages, may be had in One Vol., 6s., or in 3 Parts, 2s. 6d. each.

English Grammar and Composition. By G. A. TWENTYMAN.
Elementary. 2s. Part I. First Year 1s. 6d.
Part II. Second Year. 2s.
Part III. Middle School Composition. 3s.

English Test Papers. Junior and Senior. By A. R. FLORIAN. 1s. each.

Macaulay's Lays of Ancient Rome.
By W. EDWARDS. 2s. 6d.

Ballad and other Poetry.
Compiled by H. R. HEATLEY. 1s. 6d.

A Selection of Great Poetry.
Compiled by C. J. POWER. 2s.

A Selection of Narrative Verse.
Compiled by C. J. POWER. 2s.

NOTES

ON

BRITISH HISTORY

BY

WILLIAM EDWARDS, M.A.

HEADMASTER OF THE MIDDLESBROUGH HIGH SCHOOL
AUTHOR OF "NOTES ON EUROPEAN HISTORY"
AND "NOTES ON ENGLISH LITERATURE," ETC.

PART I

PREHISTORIC TIMES
TO RICHARD III, 1485

FIFTH EDITION
SEVENTH IMPRESSION

RIVINGTONS
34 *KING STREET*, *COVENT GARDEN*
LONDON
1927

Printed in Great Britain by T. and A. CONSTABLE LTD.
at the University Press, Edinburgh

PREFACE

It is found impossible in most English schools to devote more than two periods a week to the study of History, and teachers find considerable difficulty in doing thoroughly the work required for public examinations in the time allotted. This difficulty is increased in the case of those who attempt to deal with local records, with the development of civilisation and literature, and with contemporary European history.

The difficulty arises largely because in textbooks the chronological order is usually followed, and events and movements of considerable duration are treated not as wholes, but as portions of the reigns over which they extend. The adequate treatment of such subjects involves oral teaching, and either the dictation of notes in school or the copying of notes by the scholar out of school. The former plan unduly encroaches upon the short time available for actual teaching, the latter trespasses upon leisure time already seriously limited by home work.

These notes have been compiled in order to supplement the information given in the textbook and to lessen the amount of time devoted in school to the mere giving of notes. An attempt has been made to treat each subject fully (this has necessitated a certain amount of repetition), to bring out clearly the leading principles involved and to indicate the exact part played by the actors. The notes are supplemented by references; those under heading A being to the standard histories and biographies which may be found in any well-equipped public library; those under B to short passages of prose or poetry suitable for reading aloud to the class and not included under A; those under C to historical novels and tales suitable for the scholar's private reading. But it is not intended entirely to obviate the writing of notes by the scholars, and there are some obvious omissions which must be rectified in class, while it is clearly impossible to give in a book like this any information on local history, the study of which adds greatly to the reality and interest of the general subject. No plans, maps, or architectural illustrations have been included, and it is suggested that these should be copied into the scholar's notebook (in the case of the last with the co-operation of the art master), and that they should not be merely consulted in a textbook or atlas as occasion arises.

The notes comply, to a considerable extent, with the suggestions of the Board of Education as to the teaching of History, and are suitable for the Advanced Examinations of that Board. They deal with the leading events of contemporary European History, with the development of the Constitution, and with industry and agriculture. They may be used as headings for essays, and the references " A " will afford further material for the " practice in original composition " upon which the circular lays stress. An attempt has been made to select the most important questions and to indicate their chief features by means of the main headings. At the same time the sub-headings give fuller information for those who wish to study the subject in greater detail.

These notes are intended mainly for the use of scholars preparing for History Scholarships at the Universities, for the Oxford and Cambridge Higher Local, Higher Certificate, and Senior Local Examinations, for the Honours and Senior Certificates of the Central Welsh Board, Civil Service Examinations, the Irish Intermediate, the Scottish Leaving

Certificates, the First Class of the College of Preceptors, the Civil Service, the Matriculation, Intermediate, and Pupil Teacher Examinations. It is obvious that much of the information given will be beyond the capacity of candidates for Junior Examinations, but it is hoped that the author's *Junior British History Notes* may prove useful for these.

In a number of schools it is not possible to find room on the staff for a specialist in History, and it is hoped that these notes, which are the result of considerable experience in teaching, may be found suggestive and helpful to form masters taking the subject whose main interest lies in other parts of their work. While these Notes have been compiled mainly for use in schools, they may prove useful to those who, while not engaged in teaching, are interested in recent history.

The author would welcome any suggestions for the correction and improvement of this book. He gladly acknowledges the kindness of Mr. J. C. Scott, M.A., of King Edward VII School, Sheffield, and of Mr. S. Scruton in revising and correcting Part I.

W. EDWARDS.

HIGH SCHOOL,
    MIDDLESBROUGH.

PREFACE TO SECOND EDITION

THE author gratefully acknowledges the help received in the revision of these Notes from Rev. A. B. Beavan, M.A., of Leamington, and Mr. A. M. Walmsley, M.A., of the High School, Middlesbrough.

Professor Oman's *England before the Norman Conquest*, and Mr. H. W. C. Davis' *England under the Normans and Angevins*, should be added to the references for their respective periods.

PREFACE TO THIRD EDITION

The Author gratefully acknowledges the very valuable suggestions and corrections received for the early part of the book from Professor Haverfield, of Oxford, and Mr. W. S. Robinson, Author of " An Illustrated History of England," etc.

CONTENTS

NOTES ON BRITISH HISTORY

PREHISTORIC TIMES

I. The Men of the Stone Age.

A. Palæolithic (Old Stone-workers).

Cave-dwellers, using unpolished stone weapons; apparently had no domestic animals; ignorant of metals, weaving, and pottery, but possessing some artistic ability which enabled them to make rough drawings of animals on rock or bone. Their remains and those of tropical animals (hyenas, rhinoceros) found in caves at Brixham in Devonshire and Kirkdale in Yorkshire.

Palæolithic men destroyed by the descent of glaciers from Scandinavia as far as the Thames valley.

B. Neolithic (New Stone-workers).

Lived after the ice-deluge. Used polished flint weapons. They were able to cultivate land, make pottery, and weave cloth, but had no artistic sense. Built Stonehenge for sun-worship (Stonehenge[1] is not Druidical). Built houses, often in lakes for security; not cave-dwellers.

These men of the Stone Age were a short, dark race, which was spread over the west and south of Europe, and still forms a large proportion of the population of Northern Spain, Southern France, and Northern Italy and survives in Wales and the Highlands of Scotland. They buried their dead in long barrows.

[1] Authorities differ as to the exact purpose of Stonehenge. Some regard it as sepulchral, others as a temple of sun-worshippers.

B

II. The Celts.

A. Gaels or Goidels.—The Bronze Age.

The Gaels, a different race speaking a different language, overcame the men of the Stone Age owing to the superiority of bronze over stone weapons.

A tall, fair race ; possibly from Northern Germany ; bronze-workers. A short-headed people, mainly hunters, burying their dead in round barrows. Driven to Ireland (the Welsh word for Irish is " Gwyddel ") and the Highlands by the Cymri or Brythons.

B. Cymri or Brythons.—The Iron Age.

Drove the Goidels to the West of England, to the Highlands of Scotland, and to Ireland. Opposed the landing of Cæsar in Kent. A more civilised race. Skilled workers in iron, tin[1] (in Cornwall), and gold. Pytheas of Marseilles, about 330 B.C., noted the large corn crops of the Brythons who traded with the Phœnicians. (The " Long Ships " rocks off Land's End are called after the long trading vessels of the Phœnicians.) The Cymri were driven westward in their turn by the English, and their old name is kept in Cymry (Welsh name for " Wales ") and Cumberland.

The Cymri were organised in tribes ; had no large towns, but forest villages. Their religion was Druidism, involving a belief in the immortality of the soul (shown by food, weapons, and utensils placed in barrows for use of the souls of the dead) and human sacrifices. The Druids priests, judges, and teachers.

C. The Celts did not extinguish the Iberians, but used them as slaves ; and longer skulls found in later Celtic barrows prove intermarriage between the two races.

References :

A. *Early Man in Britain*, Boyd Dawkins, chaps. VII, VIII, X.

B. *Cæsar's Gallic War*, Book V, chaps. XII–XIV.

---

[1] The Cassiterides or Tin Islands of the Phœnicians are usually identified with the Scilly Islands. But no tin is found on the Scilly Islands, which have probably been separated from the mainland since the period in question. " Cassiter Street," in Bodmin, like the Cassiterides, is derived from κασσίτερος (tin), a Greek word of Phœnician origin.

THE ROMANS IN BRITAIN

I. **Julius Cæsar.**

  A. **55 B.C.** Landed, probably near Deal, with 10,000 men to punish the Britons for aiding the Gauls, with whom they were connected by ties of kindred and religion. Lack of cavalry prevented a decisive victory. The season was too late for a long campaign. The Roman fleet was shattered by a storm. Cæsar returned to Gaul. His first expedition, a reconnaissance in force rather than an invasion, was a failure.

  B. **54 B.C.** Came with 20,000 soldiers and 2000 cavalry. His 800 vessels formed the largest fleet that has ever attacked this country. His landing was unopposed through fear of his large force. Attempt of Cassivelaunus, King of the Catuvellauni, to unite all the British tribes against Cæsar, but owing to the opposition of the Trinobantes, and a victory of Cæsar near St. Albans (Verulamium), he submitted. Nominal submission of the Britons.

  Cæsar did not ensure the permanent conquest of Britain, but his expeditions were of great value owing to the information he gained about the Britons. Britain was not attacked for about one hundred years, owing to the rising of the Gauls against Cæsar, to civil wars in Rome, and the necessity of defending the northern and eastern frontiers of the Empire against the barbarians.

II. **The Roman Conquest.**

  A. **A.D. 43.** Aulus Plautius was sent by the Emperor Claudius to conquer Britain on the death of Cunobelinus (Shakespeare's Cymbeline), King of the Trinobantes, whose son Caratacus [Welsh "Caradog," hence not Caractacus] renounced his father's friendship with Rome. Capture of Colchester (Camulodunum), the stronghold of Caratacus, and submission of the greater portion of Britain, that is most of the land south of a line from the Humber to the Mersey.

B. A.D. **51.**   Ostorius Scapula.

> Caratacus fled to the Silures of South Wales. Was defeated at Caer Caradog (?) in Shropshire. by Scapula. Betrayed by Cartimandua, Queen of the Brigantes, to the Romans, and saved from execution by Claudius owing to his manly bearing in captivity. Fortresses were built by the Romans at Chester (Deva), Caerleon (Isca Silurum), and Wroxeter (Viroconium), to keep the frontiers.

C. A.D. **59.**   Suetonius Paulinus.

> (1) Conquered Mona (Anglesea), the centre of the Druids. Destroyed their sacred groves.
>
> (2) Great British rising, led by Boadicea [more correctly Boudicca], Queen of the Iceni, due to
>
>> a. Oppression and extortion of Roman officials.
>>
>> β. The seizure by the Romans, on failure of male heirs, of the kingdom of their ally, her husband, Prasutagus; scourging of his widow Boadicea; ill-treatment of his daughters.
>
> Union of the Trinobantes and Iceni. Capture of Camulodunum (inadequately fortified by the over-confident Romans), Verulamium, Londinium [first mention of London in history]. Destruction of IX Legion and slaughter of 70,000 Romans and friendly Britons.
>
> The rising put down with great cruelty by Paulinus. Boadicea poisoned herself, A.D. 61.

D. A.D. **75–78.**   Julius Frontinus finally subdued the Silures.

E. A.D. **78–85.**   Julius Agricola.

> (1) Final subjugation of North Wales and first attack on North Britain.
>
>> a. The Ordovices of North Wales were routed.
>>
>> β. Re-conquest of Mona.
>>
>> γ. Final subjugation of the North of England.
>>
>> δ. Defeat of the Caledonians under Galgacus at Mons Graupius. [The Grampians owe their name to the incorrect spelling of this word.] But no final conquest of the Caledonians.

(2) Consolidation of the Roman power.

  a. Agricola was a great builder of towns and military stations, e.g. (probably) Eboracum.

  β. The statesmen of his time civilised the Britons. The luxury of the towns attracted wealthy Britons, and Agricola did much to introduce the Roman language and learning. He taught the Britons to build towns and to make roads, and introduced improved methods of agriculture. Thus the Britons were reconciled to the Roman supremacy.

  γ. Fair assessment of tribute and of the corn tax.

  δ. Building of a line of forts between the Clyde and Forth.

(3) Agricola was recalled by Domitian because of pressing danger on the Danube, and owing to disapproval of his aggressive policy in Britain. The Roman authority was not effective north of the Tweed.

F. Thus the Roman Conquest was due partly to lack of union between the different tribes of Britain. It was accomplished with difficulty owing to the bravery of the resistance and the natural difficulties of the country.

III. The Roman Occupation.

A. Chronological Summary.

  c. A.D. **122.** Hadrian built a stone wall 73½ miles long, 17 feet high, 7 feet wide, strengthened by fortified camps from Wallsend to Bowness. A garrison of perhaps 10,000 protected "Hadrian's Wall" from the Caledonians (page 8, 8,a).

  c. A.D. **142.** Antoninus Pius built a turf wall from the Forth to the Clyde.

  c. A.D. **210.** Severus repaired and strengthened Hadrian's Wall. He died at Eboracum (York), **211.**

  A.D. **210–288.** Weakening of the Roman Empire owing to internal dissensions and the attacks of the barbarians.

A.D. **288**. Carausius, said by some to have been Count of the Saxon Shore,[1] profiting by the weakness of the Empire, proclaimed himself "Emperor of Britain."

A.D. **293**. Carausius assassinated by Allectus, who became "Emperor of Britain."

A.D. **296**. Constantius created Emperor of the West (Gaul, Spain, and Britain) by Diocletian, slew Allectus and restored the supremacy of Rome.

A.D. **306**. Constantius died. His son Constantine proclaimed Emperor by the soldiers at York.

A.D. **383**. Maximus greatly weakened the Roman power in Britain by withdrawing a large number of Roman soldiers to support his attempt to win the Empire.

A.D. **409**. Further depletion of Roman forces in Britain by the usurper Constantine, who used them on the Continent to support his attempt to secure the Imperial dignity.

A.D. **410**. Final refusal of Honorius, owing to the attack of the Goths under Alaric on Rome, to reinforce the depleted Roman garrison in Britain.

B. The character and results of the occupation.

(1) It was largely but not exclusively a military occupation, especially in the north and west; there was no general introduction of full Roman civic life. Only four "coloniae" (Gloucester, Lincoln, York, Colchester), and one "municipium" (Verulamium) were established. The Roman roads were military. After the withdrawal of the Romans their military system was probably retained to some extent by the Romano-British, and this may partly account for their stubborn resistance to the Anglo-Saxons.

(2) But there was a great increase in the number of towns and of commerce owing to the Pax Romana, and in the towns many buildings—temples, baths, and houses— were constructed. London became a commercial centre.

[1] The shore from the Wash to Spithead attacked, *not* colonised, by the Saxons.

(3) Great importance of "villae" or estates owned by Romans and tilled by British slaves. Freeman asserts the absolute destruction of this system after the Romans left. Seebohm sees in it the origin of the feudal manor, but this is doubtful, as the Roman villae, unlike the feudal manors, were not universal, and Celtic villages were in the majority ; further, the Anglo-Saxon hundred courts, which all the freemen attended, cannot be reconciled with the Roman villa, where all were in subjection to one man.

(4) The construction of Roman roads. Although originally made for military purposes, they greatly facilitated the growth of commerce. Three of the chief were—

    α. Dover, London, St. Albans, Viroconium, Chester. "The Watling Street."[1]

    β. Exeter, Lincoln. "The Foss Way."[1]

    γ. London, Lincoln, Aldborough, Carlisle, Newcastle. "The Ermine Street,"[1] subsequently "The Great North Road."

(5) Development of the arts of peace : Agriculture, Britain became "the Granary of the West." Lead-mining in Derbyshire and elsewhere, and tin and iron-mining (less important) in Cornwall and the Weald. Draining of marshes, clearing of forests.

(6) Introduction of Latin language and culture, higher civilisation, and greater trade owing to closer connection with the Continent. The Latin words strata, colonia, castra, portus, are found in place names *Strat*ford, Lin*coln*, Don*caster*, *Port*smouth.

(7) Introduction of new religions.

    α. Christianity.

        Little definite information. Probably introduced by Christian soldiers from Gaul. Some relics, e.g. a Christian church at Silchester. Spread in the second century, and was the leading religion in Britain in the third century, in spite of the Diocletian persecution, during which a

[1] These names were not Roman.

soldier, Albanus, is said to have suffered martyrdom, A.D. 304, at St. Albans, which took its name from him. Christian bishoprics were founded at London and York, and the Church was regularly organised. Pelagius, the founder of the Pelagian heresy (which denied the doctrine of original sin) was a Briton.

β. Many evidences of Mithraic worship. This was Oriental sun-worship typified by figures of a young man and a bull (perhaps an indication of the passage of the sun into Taurus).

γ. Roman Paganism.

(8) No complete occupation of the Island.

α. For a short time some land was occupied north of Agricola's forts, but Hadrian's wall was the practical boundary after A.D. 180 of the Roman power.

β. Wales never thoroughly conquered. It remained Celtic, and never became Roman, like Gaul.

1. Very few Roman remains in Wales.

2. The Roman roads unimportant.

3. The Welsh language continued and was very little affected by Latin.

References:

A. *The Political History of England to 1066*, Dr. Hodgkin,
B. *Boadicea,* by Cowper.　　　　　　　　　　[pp. 54-8.
C. *Beric the Briton,* by Henty, Blackie and Co.
Puck of Pook's Hill, by Rudyard Kipling.

THE ENGLISH CONQUEST

The Teutons repeatedly attacked Britain in the fourth and first half of the fifth centuries, and the Romans appointed counts of the Saxon Shore to resist their attacks. A.D. 429, Germanus, Bishop of Auxerre, sent to Britain to oppose the Pelagian heresy, helped the Britons to gain the "Hallelujah Victory" over Saxons and Picts in Yorkshire or the North Midlands. Armorica, now colonised by Britons fleeing from the Saxon attacks, received the new name of Brittany.

I. **The Jutes**—the smallest of the three tribes. Little is known of them. The general opinion that they came from Jutland is doubted by some writers who give Friesland as their original home.

   A. The Conquest of Kent.

      449.[1] The Jutes, led by Hengist and Horsa, landed at Ebbsfleet in Kent, probably at the invitation of Vortigern, and defeated the Picts and Scots.

      455. Vortigern defeated by the Jutes at Aylesford. Horsa slain. Hengist became King of Kent, and won the battle of Crayford.

      465. Final conquest of Kent at Wippedsfleet, in spite of the brave resistance of the Britons.

   B. The Jutes conquered the Isle of Wight in 530, but it soon passed into the power of Cerdic, who probably co-operated at its capture.

II. **The Saxons**—originally inhabited Holstein, but had spread over Brunswick, Hanover, and Westphalia.

   A. The Conquest of Sussex.

      491. The South Saxons, under Aelle and Cissa (cf. *Chi*chester), captured Anderida, "nor was there one Briton left alive," and established the Kingdom of Sussex.

   B. The Conquest of Essex.

      500. The Kingdom of Essex founded by the East Saxons, who later captured London.

   C. The Conquest of Wessex.

      (1) The foundation by Cerdic.

      519. Cerdic, by the victory of Charford, conquered Hampshire, assumed the title of King, and laid the foundation of the Kingdom of Wessex (but see page 235).

      But 520 the West Saxons were routed at Mount Badon (near Bath) by the Britons under Arthur. [A historical personage, but the Arthurian legend is due to the twelfth-century tales of Geoffrey of Monmouth.]

      About 530 Cerdic gained the Isle of Wight.

[1] The dates usually given have been retained, although the accuracy of some has been questioned, e.g. Dr. Hodgkin gives **441**, not **449**, as the date of the landing of the Jutes.

(2) Expansion to the East and North.

568. Ceawlin routed the Jutes at Wimbledon and conquered Surrey. Later he conquered Bucks and Bedfordshire.

(3) Expansion to the West. Checked temporarily at Mount Badon 520.

552. Cynric won the battle of Old Sarum and conquered Wiltshire, and, after a victory at Barbury (North Wilts), Berkshire.

577. By a victory at Deorham (near Bath), Ceawlin gained much of Gloucestershire and Somersetshire, and greatly strengthened Wessex by separating the Britons of Wales (the North Welsh) from those of Cornwall and Devon (the West Welsh).

Thus the Kingdom of Wessex was firmly established in spite of the defeat of Ceawlin at Feathanlea (site doubtful, probably not Faddiley in Cheshire) by the Britons in 584.

III. **The Angles**—lived about the mouth of the Elbe.

500–540. Angles established themselves in East Anglia and Lincolnshire, conquered Yorkshire and settled around the Tweed. Dum*fries* probably commemorates this Frisian settlement. The name of Angle-land or England is derived from the Angles.

547. Ida established the Kingdom of Bernicia (from the Tees to the Forth) with its capital at Bamborough.

547–580. Settlement of the northern part of the Trent valley by the Southumbrians. Settlement of the middle English round Leicester. Settlement of the West English (or Mercians, the men of the march or border) in Northants and Staffs. The beginning of Mercia.

IV. **The General Character of the Conquest.**

A. A national migration, including slaves, flocks, and herds, due probably to the conquest of the Baltic coast by the Huns, and involving the transference of Teutonic life and customs. This is proved by

(1) The importance of the family which, in England as in Germany, was the basis of society ; the family was held responsible for the crimes of each member and compensation for injuries done to each member (e.g. Weregild compensation for murder) was paid to the family.

(2) The maintenance of the division of the people into the three classes of nobles, free, and slaves, as in Germany. But the need of a military leader tended to the early establishment of monarchy in all the tribes in England. " War begat the King."

(3) German laws were retained.

(4) The system of common cultivation was retained by the village communities.

B. The stubborn resistance of the Britons made conquest slow.

(1) The Conquest of Kent took thirty years.

(2) Successes of the Britons at Mount Badon **520** and Feathanlea **584**.

(3) Wales was never conquered. West Wales and Cumberland held out for many years owing to the bravery of the Goidels (less enervated by the Roman civilisation than the Brythons) and the mountains of the West.

(4) The conquest of Hampshire and the Isle of Wight was the limit of Cerdic's success, and the foundation of Wessex took nearly one hundred years.

C. There was little cohesion between successful tribes. England was not really united until the Norman Conquest.

D. General destruction of surviving Romano-British institutions. England became heathen, and Christianity survived only in Wales.

E. The great importance of the self-governing village communities—agricultural settlements united by the bond of kindred and suited to the needs of the Anglo-Saxons, who disliked towns. Consequent decrease in the importance of towns.

F. Fusion of Anglo-Saxons and Britons.

   (1) Freeman asserts that the Britons were exterminated.

      a. The language and institutions of England are
         largely Teutonic.

      β. The slaughter at Anderida 491 supports this
         theory.

   (2) But others assert that, while the Teutonic element
       was predominant, the Britons were not exterminated.

      a. The slaughter at Anderida was specially men-
         tioned because exceptional, and only the
         garrison suffered.

      β. The British women became wives of the con-
         querors (although in Germany the latter had
         abstained from intermarriage with other races).

      γ. The few British words found in English relate
         to household needs (e.g. rug, basket, rasher),
         and warrant the belief that many Britons
         were kept as slaves. No British words relating
         to government have been retained in English.

      δ. The different types of skulls found in Saxon
         burying-places prove the amalgamation of the
         two races.

   (3) But the disappearance of Romano-British law and in-
       stitutions and of the well-organised Christianity of the
       Britons suggests that the Britons who survived were
       generally merely scattered units. But in Wessex an
       organised Celtic community, arranged in different
       ranks and possessing its own estates, existed side by
       side with the Saxons.

References :

   A. *Short History of the English People*, J. R. Green, pp. 1–16.
      Freeman's *Norman Conquest*, Vol. I, pp. 9–18.

   C. *Uther and Igraine*, by Deeping, Grant Richards.

THE STRUGGLE FOR SUPREMACY

I. **Kent.**

A. King Ethelbert (ruled from **561-616**) recovered from his defeat by Ceawlin of Wessex at Wimbledon, A.D. **568**, and secured the supremacy of Eastern England from Kent to the Humber. Was recognised as Brytaenwealda,[1] wielder or ruler of Britain, a title borne by the most powerful of the early English kings. His authority acknowledged by the Kings of Essex and East Anglia.

B. The introduction of Christianity.

(1) Owing to the influence of his Christian Queen Bertha, daughter of Charibert, King of Paris, he allowed St. Augustine, the envoy of Pope Gregory the Great, to land in Thanet, 597, and, after himself becoming a Christian, to settle in his capital, Canterbury.

(2) Augustine became Archbishop of Canterbury, consecrated Justus Bishop of Rochester, and Mellitus Bishop of London, which, though belonging to Essex, adopted Christianity through Ethelbert's influence.

(3) Failure of Augustine to effect union between the Roman and Welsh Churches and to reconcile their differences as to Baptism and the date of Easter.

(4) Christianity was practically confined to Ethelbert's dominions, although all the kingdoms except Sussex and Mercia were affected for a time.

C. The supremacy of Kent ended with Ethelbert's death. It had been successfully challenged during Ethelbert's life by Redwald of East Anglia, another Brytenwealda, who established his authority over central England.

D. A pagan reaction. Kent remained Christian, but London became pagan, and thus the ecclesiastical supremacy of Canterbury was confirmed.

[1] The title of " Brytaenwealda " is more correct than that of " Bretwalda," meaning "wide ruler." It is probably a translation of the Roman " Dux Britanniarum," but does not imply the continued existence from Roman times of a separate Empire of Britain, as some have stated. The title was purely honorific and not official, and was due to military success and the active support given to the Christian religion by the holder.

E. The introduction of Christianity was the great work of Kent, but Kentish Christianity was very weak, and the ultimate success of the Christian religion was due to Northumbria.

References :

A. *Political History of England to 1066*, pp. 112–29.
C. *The Shaven Crown*, by Bramston, S.P.C.K.

II. **Northumbria,** supreme from about 600–700.

A. Ethelfrith, 593–617.   A heathen king.

   (1) Maintained the union of Bernicia and Deira effected by his father Ethelric in **588.**

   (2) **603.**   By a victory at Dawston defeated Aidan, the Christian King of the Scots, and divided the Welsh of Strathclyde into two divisions.

      613.   By a victory at Chester separated the Welsh of Wales from the Welsh of Strathclyde.

   (3) **617.**   Defeated and slain by Redwald of East Anglia in alliance with Ethelfrith's brother-in-law, Edwin of Deira, at the battle of the Idle.

B. Edwin, 617–633.

   (1) The extension of Northumbria.

      a. Conquered the Isle of Man and Mona (henceforth Anglesea, i.e. the Angles' isle).

      β. Conquered the Britons of Loidis (Leeds and district).

      γ. Defeated the West Saxons.

      δ. Extended his dominions to the Firth of Forth and built Edinburgh (Edwin's borough).

      ε. Recognised as Brytenwealda.   Supreme over all England except Kent.

   (2) The introduction of Christianity.

      Edwin had married Ethelburga, daughter of Ethelbert of Kent, and allowed Paulinus to preach Christianity in Northumbria.   Roman Christianity was accepted by the

Witenagemot and Edwin was baptised at York, **627.** Rapid extension of the new religion owing to Paulinus' teaching.

(3) Edwin's reign a golden age. Peace and order were maintained in Northumbria, so that "a woman with her babe might walk scathless from sea to sea in Edwin's day."

(4) Union of Cadwallon, the Christian King of North Wales, who was anxious to regain his independence and objected to the Roman form of Christianity, with Penda, King of Mercia, the champion of heathendom, who feared the spread of Christianity and of Edwin's power.

> **633.** Edwin defeated and slain at Hatfield, near Doncaster. Temporary ruin of the Northumbrian power, separation of Bernicia and Deira, and end of Roman Christianity in the North.

C. Oswald of Bernicia, son of Ethelfrith, **635–642.**

(1) **634.** Routed Cadwallon at Heavenfield, near Hexham, and thus finally ensured Teutonic supremacy in Northern England.

(2) Union of Bernicia and Deira under Oswald, who ruled with a firm hand from Bamborough, his capital.

(3) The Re-establishment of Christianity.

> *a.* **563.** Foundation of the monastery of Iona by St. Columba, an Irish noble. Subsequent spread of Irish Christianity over Western Scotland.
>
> *β.* Oswald, after his father's death, found shelter at Iona and accepted the Irish form of Christianity.
>
> *γ.* Introduction of Irish Christianity, with Oswald's support, into Northumbria by St. Aidan, a monk of Iona, who built a monastery at Holy Island and finally established Christianity in Northumbria.

(4) **642.** Oswald defeated and slain by Penda at Maserfield or Oswestry (Oswald's tree or town). [The site

doubtful, possibly in Shropshire, but some assert it
was in Lancashire.]

D. Oswy, brother of Oswald, 642–671.

  (1) The consolidation and extension of his power.

   a. 655. Defeated and slew Penda at Winwoodfield,
    near Leeds, and thus finally crushed the power
    of heathendom.

   β. Reunited Bernicia and Deira—separated again
    after Oswestry.

   γ. Defeated the Picts and ruled from Aberdeen
    to the Wash.

   δ. Asserted his supremacy over Mercia until the
    rise of Penda's son Wulfhere.

  (2) The Synod of Whitby 664.

  Decision in favour of the adoption of the Roman
  form of Christianity.

   a. Roman Christianity adopted by Kent, East
    Anglia, and Wessex. Irish by Northumbria,
    and, less strongly, by Mercia and Essex.

   β. Roman Christianity accepted by the whole
    Christian world except the Irish, Picts, Britons,
    and some English. A contest between the
    authority of Columba and Aidan and the great
    churches of Paris, Rome, and Milan.

   γ. Roman Christianity was imperial, urban, episco-
    pal, and well organised on the lines of the
    Roman Empire. It owed much to the influence
    of Roman law and laid stress on the corporate
    unity of the Church. Irish Christianity was
    monastic, tribal, and loosely organised. More
    attention was paid to the individual Christian
    than to the corporate Church. The particular
    points in dispute were the date of Easter and
    the method of wearing the tonsure.

   δ. Oswy's queen, Eanfled, who had been brought
    up at the Kentish court, and Wilfrid, Abbot

of Ripon, supported the Roman form, and Oswy gave his decision in its favour because of the "power of the keys" given to St. Peter, and his unwillingness "to offend the saint who is the doorkeeper of heaven."

ε. The final decision was beneficial, although the Irish Church was purer, simpler, and more careless of wealth than the Roman. It brought English Christianity into close connection with the Continental learning. Uniformity of belief and worship was ensured in England, and the unity of the Roman Church, strengthened by the organising power of Theodore of Tarsus, tended to promote unity in the State.

671 Oswy died.

E. Ecfrith, son of Oswy, **671–685.**

(1) He defeated the Picts and the Mercians, but was defeated and slain by the former at Nechtansmere, **685,** by which defeat Northumbria lost all territory north of the Cheviots.

(2) His relations with the Church.

α. Theodore of Tarsus, appointed Archbishop of Canterbury **669,** did great service to the Church by organising and increasing the number of bishoprics. Hitherto there had been one bishopric to each kingdom and the bishops had been practically royal chaplains. With Ecfrith's approval Theodore divided Wilfrid's Bishopric[1] of York into three bishoprics in spite of Wilfrid's opposition, and thus asserted the supremacy of the Archbishop of Canterbury. (At the National Council of Hertford **673,** Theodore enforced discipline and ensured uniformity in the Church.)

β. Wilfrid, who had gained much influence by his support of Roman Christianity at Whitby,

---

[1] Wilfrid about 664 was appointed Bishop of York, which became the seat of the episcopate instead of Holy Isle (Lindisfarne) soon after the Synod of Whitby.

strongly opposed the division of his bishopric and was exiled by Ecfrith, who was jealous of his great wealth. (He held the abbeys of Hexham and Ripon). After Ecfrith's death he regained power and was made Bishop of Hexham. His career shows the growing importance of the wealthy ecclesiastical foundations.

γ. Ecfrith had friendly relations with St. Chad, the apostle of the Mercians, whom he appointed Bishop of York, and with St. Cuthbert of Lindisfarne.

F. The importance of Northumbria.

(1) It promoted the cause of Christianity, and the spread of Christianity extended the political power of the Northumbrian kings.

(2) It broke the power of the Britons in the north, and long resisted the pressure from the Picts.

(3) Northumbria had many great churchmen (Aidan, Wilfrid, Cuthbert, Chad) and scholars, such as the Venerable Bede of Jarrow, the author of the *Ecclesiastical History of the English Nation*, and the poet Caedmon of Whitby. This due largely to the piety and great learning of the Irish Church.

(4) The power of Northumbria was weakened by the jealousy between Bernicia and Deira, which often led to civil war, and by its division by the Cheviots. Its capital, York, was badly placed for consolidation and defence, and the kingdom was commanded by the high mountains of Scotland and Strathclyde. The defeat at Nechtansmere and a succession of weak kings ended its supremacy.

References :

A. *The Making of England*, J. R. Green, chap. VI.

C. *The Son of Aella* and *A Scholar of Lindisfarne*, by G. Hollis, S.P.C.K.

III. **Mercia**, supreme from about **700–800.**

> An Anglian settlement. Dissensions in Wessex at the end of Ceawlin's reign (**560–592**) prevented Wessex from checking the extension of Mercia over Leicester shire, Bedfordshire, and Buckinghamshire, and it became very powerful under Penda (Hatfield, **633**; Maserfield, **642**). After the death of Penda at Winwoodfield, **655**, Oswy became overlord of Mercia, but, with the decay of the power of Northumbria, Wulfhere, the Christian son of Penda, regained independence, subdued East Anglia and Essex, and conquered West Saxon territory in the Severn valley.

A. Ethelbald, **716–757.**

(1) Early successes. He defeated the West Saxons at Somerton, **733**, and established the supremacy of Mercia over all England south of the Humber. Took the title of "Rex Britanniae."

(2) **754.** Routed by the West Saxons at Burford. End of Mercian supremacy over Wessex.

B. Offa, **757–796.**

(1) The restoration of the power of Mercia.

775. Recovered Essex and Kent by a victory at Otford.

779. Defeated the West Saxons at Bensington (Oxfordshire) and gained Oxfordshire.

779. Defeated the Welsh. Captured Pengwern, now called Shrewsbury (Scrobbesbyrig, the town in the scrub or forest). Extended the Mercian boundary from the Severn to the Wye, and made Offa's dyke from Chester to Chepstow.

794. Annexed East Anglia and beheaded King Ethelbert—the great stain on his memory.

(2) Lichfield was made an archbishopric, **787**, with authority over seven southern bishoprics. An attempt to make Mercia ecclesiastically independent of Canterbury. The Archbishopric of Lichfield lasted only until **803**.

(3) Offa's importance recognised by Charlemagne, who undertook to protect English pilgrims to Rome from plunder. At Charlemagne's request, Offa sent Alcuin of York to teach the Frankish nobles. Offa himself went to Rome, and levied Peter's Pence in England to maintain an English college in Rome.

C. The Decline of Mercia.

The ultimate supremacy of Mercia was impossible owing to the lack of close union between its constituent tribes, the division of its territory by forests and fens, the permanent hostility of Wessex and the easy access afforded to enemies (especially the Danes) by its rivers.

825. Egbert of Wessex routed the Mercians at Ellandun, in Wilts, and conquered Mercia.

Reference :

A. *The Making of England*, J. R. Green, pp. 418–35.

IV. **Wessex,** supreme from about 800–900.

The ultimate success of Wessex was due to its steady expansion, the absorption of conquered territory and people, the unity of the West Saxon race, the early development of its administrative, financial, and military organisation, the absence of geographical divisions (like the Cheviots in Northumbria and the forests and fens of Mercia) and the control of London, the commercial, and Canterbury, the ecclesiastical capital of England. Wessex was an upland plain with no higher ground commanding it, and therefore hard to attack. Its capital, Winchester, was well placed, and its Welsh neighbours in Cornwall and Devon were weaker than their kinsmen in Wales and Cumberland.

A Ini, **688–726.**

(1) Ini conquered Somersetshire and built Taunton. He conquered Kent, Essex, and London.

(2) Ini's Laws, published about **693.**

    a. Recognised the three-field system, by which the community possessed three districts growing wheat one year, oats the second, and lying fallow the third. The ceorls, land-owning freemen, possessed and cultivated separate strips of land in each district.

β. Made provision for the protection of forests.

γ. Regulated the amount of weregild payable for murder, according to the status of the murdered man, whether English or Briton.

δ. Show that Wessex was regularly organised into shires and hundreds.

B. Egbert, 802–839.

While Offa lived Wessex was humbled, and Egbert fled from Wessex to Charlemagne's court. After Offa's death he became King of Wessex.

(1) Military successes.

α. Defeated the Welsh of Cornwall. The Tamar now the western boundary of Wessex.

β. 825. Routed the Mercians at Ellandun, and established his authority over East Anglia, Kent, Essex, and London, previously subject to Mercia. End of the supremacy of Mercia and of the long rivalry between Wessex and Mercia.

γ. Submission of Northumbria without any fighting.

δ. 837. Egbert defeated the allied forces of the Danes and West Welsh at Hengsdown Hill in Cornwall.

(2) Egbert derived additional power from his friendly relations with the Archbishop of Canterbury.

As the result of the struggle between the Anglo-Saxon kingdoms, Wessex became supreme, and the power of Wessex was established in time to offer effective resistance to the Danes—a task too great for Mercia or Northumbria. But Egbert, although his suzerainty was recognised by the whole country, did not unite England. The old royal houses continued in Northumbria and Mercia, and the rivalry between different kingdoms weakened the opposition to the Danes.

During the struggle for supremacy, and as the result of the absorption of smaller kingdoms by Northumbria, Mercia, and Wessex, the power of the King was greatly increased, the Witenagemot became a royal and not a national council,[1] and the Thegns, originally the King's personal followers, became very important, owing to the large grants of land with which their services were rewarded.

References :

A. *The Making of England*, J. R. Green, pp. 386–93 and 434–6

THE DANES

I. General.

A. The poverty of their country and the growing population made piracy the regular occupation of the younger inhabitants of the united Kingdom of Norway, Sweden, and Denmark ["Northmen" a more accurate term for the early comers than "Danes"], and Europe suffered greatly from their ravages, which extended from Iceland to Antioch, e.g. modern Russia founded by Rurik 862.

---

[1] Freeman's view (followed by Green) that the Witenagemot was a democratic assembly descended from the German folkmoot described by Tacitus (Stubbs' *Charters*, p. 56, c. 11–12) is now strongly contested. In view of the number of folkmoots in England, it is difficult to derive the Witenagemot from the Wessex folkmoot alone as Freeman does, and the triple division of England into Wessex, Mercia, and the Danelagh precludes the possibility of one folkmoot for the whole country before the Norman Conquest. The English Witenagemot was probably an oligarchic assembly descended from the *concilium principis* of Tacitus, and it acted as the privy council of the King. It numbered usually about thirty, and on great occasions about a hundred. The ex-officio members, e.g. the ealdormen and bishops, attended regularly, but the Thegns attended only by special summons. The powers of the Witan were vague and undefined, varying according to the personality of the King. The King was probably not elected by the Witan, but chosen by the other members of the royal family, and accepted by the chief men individually, not acting as "a national council." A grant of folk-land (not common land belonging to the people, but land held by folkright, i.e. customary law) was made by the King, and the signatures of members of the Witenagemot found on deeds of transfer are not proofs of the concurrence of that body in the grant, but merely the acts of legal witnesses to the deed.

B. The Northmen were most skilful sailors (their boats had no deck, only one mast, and were only four feet deep) and metalworkers (using the iron of Sweden for their armour and axes). On land they used captured horses to facilitate rapid movement, and strengthened their position by cleverly constructed earthworks.

C. England was an easy prey, owing to disunion, lack of an organised army, navy, and strong forts, easy access into the interior by rivers.

D. The treasures of the churches and monasteries were a great attraction to the pagan Northmen.

II. The Danish Attack.

A. The period of plundering raids followed by speedy return home. Early Danish attacks on Ireland (Danish settlements founded later at Dublin and Waterford) and Western Scotland.

c. 790. First attack on Wessex.

793. The Danes attacked Northumbria.

837. The Danes in alliance with the West Welsh defeated by Egbert at Hengsdown Hill.

845. Defeated by Osric the Ealdorman and Eahlstan Bishop of Sherborne at the mouth of the Parret.

852. Defeated at Ockley (Surrey) by Ethelwulf.

B. The period of raids followed by settlement in England, due to the growing power of the Frankish kings which made attacks on Frankish lands more difficult, and of central authority in Denmark restraining turbulent nobles.

855. The Danes wintered in Sheppey. The first winter they spent in England.

Attacks on various kingdoms.

(1) 867. Conquest of Deira by Halfdene. York the Danish capital. Yorkshire shows more traces of Danish occupation than other parts of England in dialect, in the political division into ridings and wapentakes, in place names, and in the physical characteristics of the people.

(2) **868.**   The Danes attacked Mercia.

(3) **870.**   Conquest of East Anglia.   The Chronicle states that Saint Edmund was slain in battle (not shot by Danish archers as legend asserts).

(4) **871.**   "The year of battles."   First attack on Wessex from a fortified camp at Reading.   Victories of Alfred at Ashdown and Wilton.   Failure of the Saxons to prevent the retreat of the defeated Danes to Reading, but owing to these defeats the Danes withdrew from Wessex.

(5) **874.**   Conquest of Mercia.

(6) **875.**   Conquest of Bernicia by Halfdene.

(7) Second attack on Wessex.

877.   Flight of Alfred to Athelney (where he did *not* burn the cakes).

877.   The Danes defeated at Exeter.   Their leader Ubba slain.

878.   Repeated attacks on Wessex from the Danish Camp at Chippenham.   The Danes routed at Ethandune and the camp at Chippenham captured by Alfred. The capture of their base of operations led to the withdrawal of the Danes from Wessex according to the terms of the Treaty of Wedmore.   Guthrum became a Christian.

(8) Third attack on Wessex.

886.   Alfred routed Guthrum, who had broken the Treaty of Wedmore, captured London, and made "Alfred and Guthrum's peace," which fixed the boundary of the Danelagh "On the Thames, then up on the Lea to its source, then right to Bedford, then up on the Ouse unto Watling Street."

By this treaty Alfred gained London, Middlesex, and part of Mercia in addition to Wessex, which he had secured in 878.   The loss of the rest of England and the division of England into two parts was inevitable, but did not greatly weaken the power of Wessex, which had had little real power over the lands now included in the Danelagh. But the recognition of the Danes as owners of the Danelagh aggravated a difference which had long existed between the Anglian North and Saxon (including Jutish) South.

(9) Final attack of the Danes under Hastings due to the return from the Continent of the remains of the Danish army (routed by Arnulf at Louvain 891) helped by the Danes of the Danelagh.

894. The Danes routed at Buttington (Montgomeryshire) by the West Saxons, Mercians, and North Welsh.

897. Capture of the Danish ships in the Lea by the Londoners.

III. Effects of the Early Danish Attacks.

A. England was divided into two parts, West Saxon territory and the Danelagh.

B. The supremacy of Wessex—the nucleus of English union —was ensured by the destruction of the Kingdoms of Northumbria, Mercia and East Anglia.

C. The further growth of the kingly power and of the importance of the Thegns owing to war. The free landowning "Ceorls" become villeins through "commending" their lands to the Thegns in return for protection from the Danes. Consequent growth of Anglo-Saxon feudalism, especially after the issue of Athelstan's law that every landless man should come under the protection of a lord.

D. Overthrow of Christianity, destruction of churches and monasteries by the heathen Danes.

E. Infusion of Teutonic blood and introduction of Danish words wapentake, riding, place names in by, thwaite, thorpe.

F. Development of the foreign policy of English kings through fear of the Danes.

856. Attempt of Ethelwulf to form an alliance with Charles the Bald, King of the Franks.

925–36. Alliance of Athelstan with the Holy Roman Emperor Otto the Great and Hugh Duke of Paris.

    G. Impetus given to English maritime development

        1. By necessity of shipbuilding to resist the Danes (e.g. by Alfred).

        2. By the infusion of viking blood.

    H. Growth of towns.

        1. "Burhs" built by Edward I and Ethelfleda to withstand the Danes.

        2. Growth of trade with Scandinavia, especially in the days of Canute.

        3. The Danes showed great capacity for municipal development, e.g. in the Danish Boroughs.

Reference :

    C. *A Thane of Wessex* and *King Alfred's Viking,*
        C. W. Whistler, Blackie and Nelson.

ALFRED THE GREAT

Born **848**, at Wantage. Youngest son of Ethelwulf. Excellently trained by his mother Osburga, but the story of his learning to read at the age of six is incorrect, although he could read at the age of twelve. Twice taken to Rome in childhood. Became King **871**, died **901**.[1]

I. A Successful Warrior.

    A. He saved Wessex by his victories at Ashdown (**871**) and Ethandune (**878**), and enabled Wessex to prevent the Danes from conquering the whole of England.

    B. By his victory over Guthrum in **886** he added Middlesex, London, and Southern Mercia to Wessex.

    C. Repulsed the attack of the Danes under Hastings (**893–897**).

II. Organised and developed the military power of England.

    A. Built forts.

    B. Organised a navy. "King Alfred bade build long ships against the ashes" [the Danish viking ships].

    C. Organised the fyrd, the national army. Half to fight and half to remain at home. The value of this work was shown by the comparative ease with which Hastings was defeated.

[1] **901** is generally given as the date of Alfred's death. Probably the correct date is **899**.

III. Gave strong encouragement to learning, religion, and civilisation, which had suffered greatly through the Danish attacks. This part of Alfred's work was rendered possible by the peace he gave to Wessex.

A. Learning.

(1) Ordered the compilation of the Anglo-Saxon Chronicle.

(2) Invited to his court scholars such as Asser the Welshman, Plegmund the Mercian (afterwards Archbishop of Canterbury), Grimbald the Frank, and John the Old Saxon.

(3) Translated, with their help, Bede's *Ecclesiastical History*, the *History of Orosius* (in which he incorporated an account of Othere's voyage to the far North), the *Consolation of Philosophy*, by Boethius.

(4) Founded schools.

B. Religion.

(1) Founded churches and monasteries.

(2) Translated Pope Gregory's *Regula Pastoralis* (duty of a pastor) for the instruction of the clergy.

C. Civilisation and trade benefited by the encouragement of Alfred, who patronised merchants and explorers (e.g. Othere) and brought foreign craftsmen into England

IV. A Great Lawgiver.

He re-enacted Ini's Laws, but modified them by applying much of the Mosaic Law and the teachings of Christianity. His laws inflict less severe punishments than those of Ini, and this was due partly to the "mildheartedness" of the King and partly to the rise in value of the precious metals owing to the Danish ravages and the consequent decrease in the amount of fines inflicted. He recognised the importance of the folkmoots, but his recognition of the right of private war on failure of justice showed that the central power could not afford justice in all cases.

V. A devout Christian, consciously aiming at the moral and
material improvement of his people and carrying on his
great work in spite of continuous illness. Called
" Wessex's Darling" by the Chronicler.

References :

A. *The Conquest of England*, by J. R. Green, chap. IV.

B. *God Save King Alfred*, by Gilliat, Macmillan.

THE DANES—ALFRED TO EDGAR

The conquest of the Danelagh imperative. At every crisis in
Wessex the Danes attacked. They supported pretenders to the
West Saxon throne, e.g. Ethelwald against Edward the Elder.
The tenth century saw the conquest of the Danelagh, the extension
of West Saxon power, the completion of Alfred's work, and the
recovery of England for the English. During this century the
Anglo-Saxon monarchy attained its highest point of power.

I. Edward the Elder (901–925).

A. Attack on the Danelagh. He "abandoned the older strategy
of battle and raid for that of siege and fortress building."
Ethelfleda, Lady of the Mercians, attacked the Danelagh, conquered the five Danish boroughs (a confederacy
with separate earls and separate hosts), built forts at
Derby and Leicester. She conquered the Welsh (built
forts at Chirk and Brecon), and strengthened her power
on the border (built forts at Shrewsbury and Bridgenorth). Died **918.**

Edward the Elder completed his sister's work. He
conquered the East Midlands (built a fort at Bedford);
Essex; Lincs (built a fort at Stamford); Notts (built a
fort at Nottingham); S. Lancs (built a fort at Man-
chester).

Thus forts extended from the Blackwater to the Lea,
Lea to Ouse, Ouse to Dee and Mersey.

B. Edward was actual King up to the Humber and Overlord of North Wales, Northumbria, and Strathclyde. The King of the Scots acknowledged him as "father and lord," and the subjection of Scotland, asserted later, was incorrectly based upon this, although the acknowledgment meant only that the Scots were the subject allies of Edward the Elder *himself*, and no more.

II. **Athelstan became "Lord of the whole of Britain" 925–940.**

A. Development of foreign policy, partly through common danger from the Danes. His sisters married Otto the Great (Holy Roman Emperor), Charles the Simple (King of the Franks), and Hugh the Great, Duke of Paris. Louis d'Outremer, son of Charles the Simple, took refuge in Athelstan's court, also Hakon, afterwards King of Norway.

B The growing power of Athelstan led to the combination of two Christian and two heathen kings—"a determined attempt to ruin Wessex"—formed by Constantine, King of the Scots, together with the King of Strathclyde and two heathen Danish kings from Ireland, where the Danes had become very strong. Routed at Brunan-
937. burgh [probably in Dumfriesshire, possibly Cheshire, not Bourne, in Lincolnshire, as some suggest].

C. Athelstan supreme over England, with vague authority over all Britain. " Rex Anglorum curegulus totius Britanniæ." Also took the title of Basileus. Subordinate Kings of Wales and Scotland attended his court and attested his charters.

D. Domestic Policy.
   (1) Public order was maintained. In London the Frith Guild, a voluntary association of men in hundreds and tithings, provided for the mutual defence of its members and the pursuit of thieves.
   (2) Extension of the shire system of Wessex to Mercia and East Anglia.

III. **Edmund and Edred.**

945. Edmund ravaged Cumberland and let it to Malcolm,
King of Scotland, on condition "that he should be his
fellow-worker both on sea and land." This did not
involve the supremacy of England over Scotland, but was
merely an acknowledgment of subordination to Edmund.

954. Rising of the Danes of the North against Edred. Attempt
to establish Eric of Norway as King of Northumbria,
supported by Wulfstan, Archbishop of York (a Dane),
whose accession to the archbishopric shows the growing
fusion of Danes and Saxons. Failed. Final end of the
separate kingdom of Northumbria, which was now
given to Oslac as Earl, not King, and completion of
the submission of the country to Wessex—the work
of Alfred's house. Therefore

IV. Edgar the Pacific was " Cæsar totius Britanniæ." The story of
the seven kings who rowed King Edgar's boat probably
true (but may have happened at Caerlon-upon-Usk rather
than Chester), and involved an acknowledgment of his
supremacy.

References :

A. *Conquest of England,* by J. R. Green, chap. v.
B. *Battle of Brunanburgh,* Tennyson.
C. *Thorstein of the Mere,* by Collingwood, E. Arnold.

DUNSTAN, A.D. c. 925–988

I. **Early Life.**

Born at Glastonbury about 925, of good family
Cruelly treated by the young nobles at Athelstan's court,
and therefore retired to Glastonbury, where he became
a monk. Made Abbot of Glastonbury by Edmund.
Exiled by Edwy, whose marriage with his cousin he
had opposed, but recalled by Edgar, who made him
Bishop of Worcester and London. 960–988 he was Archbishop of Canterbury and the leading man in England.

II. Ecclesiastical Policy.

A. A great moral reformer. Insisted on the strict Benedictine rule which had been established at the Abbey of Clugny in Burgundy (poverty, chastity, obedience, silence, long fasts). He expelled from the monasteries the "canonici" (an inferior order not bound to renounce property), and restored Benedictine regular monks. Strongly opposed the marriage of the clergy, and compelled many married secular clergy (parish priests) to put away their wives. Restored much Church property to the monasteries.

B. A patron of learning and a great teacher. He helped the Church to recover from the effects of the Danish ravages.

III. Dunstan's Political Work.

His influence was supreme under Edred and Edgar, and he was largely responsible for the policy of these kings.

A. The Danes, 954. Rising in Northumbria (under Wulfstan, Archbishop of York, aiming at the establishment of a Danish kingdom) crushed, but the government of Northumbria entrusted to Oslac, a Dane, "as earl, not king."

But Dunstan allowed much independence of law and custom to the Danelagh, and established earldoms which tended to perpetuate the national jealousy of the Anglo-Saxon kingdoms.

B. In Wessex he established firm government. The hundred courts were reorganised.

C. A fleet was equipped to guard the coast.

D. Commerce was encouraged.

IV. The Importance and Character of Dunstan.

A. A great ecclesiastical statesman, like Becket and Wolsey. He did much to ensure the general recognition of Edgar the Pacific (e.g. by the kings who rowed him on the Dee), but the growing power of the great nobles and the continuance of local jealousy were sure to lead to disunion under a weak king. This was shown during Dunstan's life.

(1) The quarrel between Dunstan and Edwy was due largely to quarrels between the King and his thegns.

(2) The murder of Edward the Martyr was probably due to some obscure difference between political parties.

The general chaos that followed Dunstan's death shows the value of his work in maintaining peace and order, but his action in setting up great earldoms introduced an element of division which greatly weakened England.

B. **A** great craftsman. A painter, harpist, designer, organ builder, and architect. The story that he contrived an accident by which his opponents were killed by the fall of part of a room at the council of Calne is quite untrue. Owing to his skill as a craftsman and to his somewhat nervous and hysterical temperament his enemies believed that he was aided by the Devil.

C. In spite of his stern measures in the cause of ecclesiastical reform he was probably a genial and lovable man, not harsh and cruel as has been generally supposed.

References :

A. *The Conquest of England*, by J. R. Green, pp. 317–58.

C. *Edwy the Fair*, by Crake, Longmans, Green, and Co.

CONQUEST BY THE DANES OF THE WEST SAXON KINGDOM

I. Decline of the Power of the Royal West Saxon House.

A. The development of Wessex was marked by centralisation without concentration. Local jealousy (especially between Mercia and Wessex) continued and united opposition to the Danes became impossible.

B. Later West Saxon kings were unable to give strong leadership.

(1) The seeds of decay were probably sown in Edgar's pacific reign, when a considerable measure of local government was given to various parts of the country.

(2) Edward the Martyr died young, probably the victim of his step-mother's hatred.

(3) Ethelred II the Unready (Redeless—the man who lacked good advice) was utterly incompetent. He showed an unrivalled genius for failure, and was sensual and degraded. The old royal stock of Cerdic was becoming exhausted. Ethelred

    α. Failed to make a navy, to reorganise the fyrd, to unite the forces of the thegns into a national army.

    β. By attempting to buy off the Danes by money raised by the Danegeld, he excited their cupidity and impoverished the country.[1]

    991.   Paid them £10,000.

    994.   Bought off Sweyn and Olaf Trygvasson, King of Norway, for £10,000.

    Dr. Hodgkin estimates the total paid as equivalent to upwards of £8,500,000 in modern money.

    γ. **1002.**   The massacre of St. Brice's day. "Not only a crime, but a blunder." Probably limited to the Danes settled in Wessex and very doubtful if, even there, there was a general massacre of women and children.

---

[1] The first levy of the Danegeld in 991 was used to hire a mercenary army of Danes to fight their own countrymen and not, as afterwards, as a bribe to induce them to withdraw from England. The Danegeld, the only direct tax of its time in Western Europe, was a land tax of, usually, a few shillings on the hide. It helped to depress the small landholding freemen (ceorls) into villeins, and was a most valuable source of revenue to the king. It lasted until 1164, and in Ethelred II's time aided the development of the central government owing to the growth of the importance of the royal "Hoarder" (Treasurer), whose office was reorganised in order to deal with the collection and management of this tax.

D

II. **Great Growth in the Power of the Ealdormen.** The original ealdormen were the governors, for the King, of the shires of Wessex ; later the ealdorman became the governor of a province comprising several shires—he presided in the various shire courts, led the shire levies, had certain official rights (e.g. to the "third penny" of the fines of the shire courts), and held official lands in addition to his large private estates. The ealdormen tended to become the private owners of their province, and their power, greatly increased by the policy of Dunstan, made them too strong to be controlled by weak kings, whose representatives they nominally were.

III. **The Weakness of the Fyrd** owing to the great depression of the agricultural population. It could have been made strong by thorough reorganisation and good leadership, as was shown by

    (1) The gallant fight of the followers of Brythnoth at Maldon, **991**, although the majority of the Essex fyrd fled.

    (2) The victory of Ulfketyl at Thetford, **1004**.

    (3) The strong defence of London, **994** and **1009**.

IV. **The Navy generally neglected.** Although in **1008** a new navy, raised by a ship tax—the precursor of later ship-money—was collected by Ethelred, it utterly failed owing to treachery to check the Danes. The coasts were left unguarded, and in **987** the Danes again began their invasions, which had ceased since Alfred's day.

V. **After the retirement of Dunstan the Church lost ground.**

VI. **The organisation of Denmark** (under Sweyn), Norway (under Olaf Trygvasson) and Sweden (under Olaf) into separate kingdoms made more dangerous the Danish attacks, which were now far better organised. Sweyn, in **1013**, changed his policy and aimed at the definite conquest of the country instead of plundering raids.

VII. **The Danes of the Danelagh** friendly to the invaders, e.g. **1013** Northumbria speedily submitted to Sweyn, who had landed in the Humber.

VIII. The resistance to the Danes was weakened somewhat by the attacks of the Welsh on Mercia.

IX. The Course of the Conquest.

991. Defeat of the Essex fyrd at Maldon. First payment of Danegeld.

994. Successful defence of London. The Danes (Sweyn and Olaf Trygvasson) withdrew on further payment.

998. The Danes settled in the Isle of Wight.

999. The Danes ravaged Kent. The failure of the English fleet may have been due to treachery.

1002. Massacre of St. Brice's Day.

1004. The victory of Ulfketyl at Thetford saved Norfolk for a time.

1008. Failure of a new navy raised by a ship-tax.

1012. Murder of Alphege, Archbishop of Canterbury.

1013. Sweyn became King.

1015–16. Gallant resistance of Edmund Ironside, a worthy descendant of Cerdic. Defeat of the Danes at Brentford; Edmund defeated by the Danes at Assandun owing to the treachery of Edric Streona. Partition of the country between Edmund and Canute.

1016. Death of Edmund. Probably due to natural causes and neither to the treachery of Edric, nor to Canute's orders, as there is no contemporary suggestion of foul play.

References :

A. *The Political History of England to 1066*, by Dr. Hodgkin, chap. XXII.

C. *King Olaf's Kinsman* and *Wulfric the Weapon Thane* Whistler, Blackie.

CANUTE, 1016–1035

Canute (son of Sweyn, who died 1014) was defeated by Edmund Ironside at Brentford, won a great victory over Edmund at Assandun in Essex, owing to the treachery of Edric Streona, and became King of all England on the death of Edmund, **1016**.

I. The Settlement of the Country.

    A. Canute strengthened the royal power.

        (1) He raised a standing army of some five thousand huscarls devoted to himself.

        (2) He nominated earls for Northumbria, East Anglia, and Mercia, but at first retained Wessex in his own hands.

        (3) Married Emma, widow of Ethelred II and sister of Richard the Fearless, Duke of Normandy, and thus lessened the danger of attack from the Continent.

    B. Crushed the family of Ethelred the Unready.

        (1) Slew Edwy, the brother of Edmund Ironside.

        (2) Sent the two sons of Edmund to the King of Sweden and asked him to murder them. They escaped to Hungary, where Edward the Outlaw married King Solomon's sister and became the father of Edgar the Atheling.

        (3) Slew Edric Streona (Ethelred's son-in-law) " very justly."

    C. Canute tried to rule as an English king, not as a foreigner.

        (1) Sent the Danish army away.

        (2) Revived Edgar's laws and made them binding on Englishmen and Danes.

        (3) Made Godwin Earl of Wessex and Leofwine Earl of Mercia. Restored the old English line in Northumbria.

        (4) Enlisted faithful Englishmen as well as Danes in the " huscarls."

(5) Canute's chapel clerks, originally household officials, were organised as a department of State, and dealt with the issue and drafting of royal writs and charters. The beginning of the "Chancery," which was at first a secretarial and not a judicial department.

D. He gave England peace, which, with the exception of the Norman conquest, lasted two hundred years. The scarcity of facts of domestic history in his reign is a sure proof of the peace of his later years, which made his visit to Rome possible. During this time churches were built and the bones of St. Alphege translated to Canterbury. Fair taxes were levied, justice administered, part of the Fens was drained, and trade prospered greatly.

II. **Canute's Foreign Policy.**

A. He wished to make England the centre of a Northern Empire. He added Norway to Denmark and England by the defeat of St. Olaf in 1028. His authority acknowledged by the Norwegian nobles whom the bribes of "Canute the Rich" had won over.

B. 1018. Malcolm of Scotland routed the Northumbrians at Carham, gained Lothian, and finally fixed the Cheviots as the boundary between England and Scotland. But in 1031 Malcolm acknowledged Canute's supremacy. (This merely an acknowledgment of Canute personally and not of his successors.)

C. 1026. Canute's visit to Rome. [Edward VII the next English King to visit Rome.] Was present at the coronation of the Holy Roman Emperor Conrad II in 1027.

Made agreements with the Pope and Emperor by which

(1) The fees payable by Archbishops going to Rome for the pallium[1] were limited.

(2) Customs dues paid by English merchants were lowered.

---

[1] The pallium was a tippet of white wool which was a sign of the Pope's acceptance of a newly appointed Archbishop.

(3) Canute undertook to enforce the strict payment in England of Peter's Pence and tithes.

(4) His daughter Gunhilda was betrothed to Conrad's son Henry (afterward the Emperor Henry III).

(5) The Eider was recognised as the boundary between Germany and Denmark. [This boundary altered by the conquest of Schleswig-Holstein by Prussia, 1864.]

III. **Canute's Character and the Value of his Work.**

A. Character. Like Octavian and Henry V his character improved with success.

(1) In early life he was cruel and ruthless.

1013. Cut off hands and noses of hostages.

1016. Tried to ensure the murder of Edmund's sons.

1025. Had his brother-in-law Ulf treacherously murdered.

(2) Later he showed himself a just, moderate, and pious ruler.

B. His work.

(1) The union of England, Norway, and Denmark, and the closer connection with the Continent, greatly stimulated trade. London became the entrepôt for goods from Northern Europe and the Mediterranean.

(2) The division of England into earldoms revived the old jealousies of the Saxon kingdoms and increased the tendency to disruption owing to the growing power of the great magnates. The union of England not restored until the Norman Conquest.

(3) He brought into prominence the family of Godwin, destined to defend England against the Normans.

References :

A. *The Conquest of England*, by J. R. Green, chap. ix.

B. J. R. Green's *Short History*, pp. 66-7.

C. *Alfgar the Dane*, by Crake, Longmans, Green, and Co.

THE FAMILY OF GODWIN

I. **Godwin**.

A. Deputy of King Canute.

Not a cowherd's son, as sometimes stated, but of good family. A successful warrior. Gained the favour of King Canute, who made him Earl of Wessex (previously kept by the King). Acted as deputy for Canute when he visited Denmark, and married Gytha, Canute's cousin. At first he was regarded as a Dane rather than a Saxon, although later he became the champion of the English. (Cf. Simon de Montfort, page 129.)

B. The Kingmaker.

On the death of Canute, Godwin at first supported Hardicanute (son of Canute and Emma), but finally united with Mercia and Northumbria to ensure the succession of Harold Harefoot, and was cognisant of, if not an accomplice in, the blinding of Alfred, son of Ethelred the Unready. Godwin supported the election of Edward the Confessor, and compelled the Queen Dowager Emma to desist from interference with the government.

C. Godwin supreme.

(1) He possessed great influence over Edward the Confessor, a weak, saintly King, who married Godwin's daughter Edith. Godwin "ruled the King and all England."

(2) Godwin and his family were supreme over all England south of a line from the Wash to Bristol.

a. Godwin, Earl of Wessex and Kent; Harold, Earl of East Anglia and Essex; Sweyn held Hereford, Gloucester, Somerset, and Berkshire; Beorn, nephew of Godwin, held Derby.

β. Godwin's power led to a revival of the old jealousy of Wessex, shown by Leofric, Earl of Mercia, and Siward the Bear, Earl of Northumbria.

D. Godwin's anti-Norman policy.

Edward had been brought up in Normandy and after his accession showed great favour to the Normans, making his nephew Ralph Earl of Hereford and Robert of Jumièges Archbishop of Canterbury. Consequent danger that the Normans would oppress the common people and prevent the English from obtaining the chief positions. Godwin, partly through selfish, partly through patriotic motives, strongly opposed the growth of Norman influence, and made an alliance with Flanders against the Normans.

E. Godwin's banishment.

Godwin, as Earl of Kent, refused to punish the citizens of Dover for an attack on Edward's brother-in-law, Eustace of Boulogne.

1051. Godwin subsequently expelled by the Witan, probably for opposition to King Edward and for complicity in the murder of Alfred. His expulsion due not only

1. To the King's anger at his anti-Norman policy, but also
2. To the fear of Godwin's family, e.g. Sweyn had carried off the Abbess of Leominster and murdered his cousin Beorn.
3. To the old jealousy of Wessex. Leofric and Siward supported the King.

During Godwin's absence William of Normandy visited Edward, who is said to have promised him the crown.

F. Godwin's return.

The support of Kent and London, and of Stigand, enabled Godwin to return. The Normans fled, and Stigand was made Archbishop of Canterbury, although

1. Robert of Jumièges was alive.
2. The Antipope Benedict X gave Stigand the pallium, and thus his position as Primate was weakened owing to lack of support of the orthodox Pope.

1053. Godwin died of apoplexy (not choked by sacred bread as the Normans asserted).

II. **Harold Godwinson.**

   A. Harold's visit to William of Normandy, **1064 (?)**.

      (1) The facts are very obscure. It is doubtful if Harold's visit was accidental or due to shipwreck, or whether, as some have held, he visited William to secure the release of some friends captured by William, or to inform William that he was to succeed Edward. (This last most improbable, as William could not succeed without the consent of the Witan, which had not been obtained.)

      (2) Harold knighted for service given to William in a war against Brittany. But it is doubtful whether he promised to marry William's daughter Adela or whether he took an oath of homage to William, and how far such an oath, if taken, was due to compulsion.

   B. Harold's accession.

      (1) Harold was of royal blood, his mother being a cousin of Canute, and Harold himself first cousin of Sweyn, King of Denmark.

      (2) A strong ruler needed. The house of Cerdic was very weak, and had been passed over at the accession of Canute.

      (3) Pope Alexander II approved of William's expedition because

            α. It was considered that Harold had broken his oath, and that William was the legal successor of Edward the Confessor.

            β. Harold had married Aldgyth (widow of Gryffydd of Wales, and granddaughter of Leofric of Mercia), and not Adela of Normandy.

            γ. He feared that, if Harold succeeded, Archbishop Stigand (ordained by the Antipope Benedict X) would weaken the connection between Rome and England, and make it difficult to check the predominance of the secular priests and the marriage of the clergy, to both of which, as an ardent supporter of the Clugniac reformation, he was strongly opposed.

            δ. William's expedition was thus a " crusade."

C. **The** Battle of Hastings.

　I. Harold's bad luck.

　　　α. Harold collected a great fleet at the Isle of Wight to oppose William. Contrary winds delayed William's arrival, and the English fleet, greatly damaged by storms, had to be dispersed.

　　　β. Harold was compelled to march north at a critical time to check Harold Hardrada (the ally of his exiled brother Tostig, Earl of Northumbria), who had defeated the English at Fulford. Victory of Harold at Stamford Bridge, where Tostig and Harold Hardrada were slain. Owing to Harold's absence in the north William landed unopposed at Pevensey, and made a strong camp at Hastings.

　　　γ. Harold was unable to secure the help of the Northumbrians (many of whom had been slain at Fulford) and Mercians at Hastings. He had to depend on the men of Wessex, East Anglia, and London, and his troops consisted largely of peasants.

　II. The battle.

　(1) The English took up a good position on a hill. Their position strengthened by a ditch and perhaps a palisade. (The character of the latter doubtful. Some say it was a regular stockade, others merely the wooden shields of the English. It may have been a rough fence intended to check cavalry.)

　(2) William won, in spite of the brave resistance of the English, because

　　　α. He was stronger in archers and cavalry.

　　　β. By feigning flight he drew the English from their position.

　　　γ. After the death of Harold and his brothers there were no leaders able to direct the English forces (and the lack of competent leaders explains the absence of a strong opposition to the Normans after Hastings).

　　　δ. His archers shot upwards and the arrows fell on the heads of the English.

(3) Dr. Delbrück (in *Numbers in History,* Hodder & Stoughton) considers that the number of men engaged at Hastings has been greatly exaggerated and estimates the Norman army at 6000–7000 and the English at 4000.

D. King Harold.

   I. Considerable military skill.

    a. **1063.** He conquered the Welsh, and the peaceful state of Wales under the Normans was partly due to him.

    β. His marches to Stamford Bridge, and subsequently to Hastings, were effected with great rapidity.

    γ. The disposition of his forces at Senlac was excellent.

   II. His power was weakened

    a. By the growing independence of Mercia and Northumbria, due partly to his conciliatory policy.

    β. By doubts as to the regularity of his succession.

    γ. By his support of Stigand.

The attempt of the house of Godwin to keep England for the English failed. Its failure was fortunate, for England benefited greatly by the Norman Conquest.

References :

A. "The Oath of Harold." Freeman's *Norman Conquest,* Vol. III, pp. 240–54. "The Character of Harold." *Conquest of England,* Appendix 2.

"The Battle of Hastings." Freeman's *Norman Conquest,* Vol. III, pp. 450–507.

C. *Harold,* by Lord Lytton.

THE NORMAN CONQUEST

I. **From the Battle of Hastings to the Coronation of William I.**

A. Edgar Atheling, son of Edward the Outlaw and grandson of Edmund Ironside, accepted as King by the magnates.

B. William captured Dover (to ensure connection with the Continent) and Canterbury. Winchester submitted.

C. William crossed the Thames at Wallingford and fixed his camp at Berkhampstead, thus isolating London and securing command of the roads from the north.

D. The magnates, seeing that further resistance was useless, offered the crown to William. Submission of Edgar Atheling and Edwin and Morcar, who had fled from London on William's approach.

E. December 25th, 1066. William I crowned by Aldred, Archbishop of York (not by Stigand, Archbishop of Canterbury), in Westminster Abbey, with all the old ritual and ceremony.

F. William granted a charter to London. A wise act which gained the strong support of the Londoners.

II. **Saxon Risings against William.**

All of these were local movements. The lack of capable Saxon leaders prevented any combined national opposition.

Due generally not to opposition to William's rule, but to the cruelty of his representatives.

A. **1067.** Rebellion in Hereford and Kent owing to the oppression of William's half-brother, Odo of Bayeux, and FitzOsbern, who acted as regents during his absence in Normandy.

B. **1068.** Exeter, where Harold's mother had taken refuge, captured.

C. **1068.** Defeat of Edwin and Morcar, conquest of Mercia, capture of York.

D. **1069.** General revolt in Northumbria under Waltheof, in alliance with Sweyn, King of Denmark, Edgar Atheling, and Malcolm Canmore, of Scotland. York captured; its Norman garrison slain.

At the same time the Welsh rose in the west. The revolt crushed.

1. No help came from Scotland.

2. William bribed Sweyn to withdraw the Danish fleet from the Humber.

3. William captured York and utterly laid waste the country from York to the Tees; 100,000 people perished, agriculture was ruined, and the district remained a desert for several centuries. The sentence "Hoc est wasta" repeatedly occurs in the Yorkshire entries in Domesday Book. "The Harrying of the North."

4. **1070.** William captured Chester and, in spite of great difficulties, led an expedition to North Wales.

5. Establishment of the earldoms of Chester and Shrewsbury to check the Welsh, and of the Palatine Bishopric of Durham to check the Scotch.

E. **1071.** Edwin killed. Hereward the Wake and Morcar submitted to William, who captured their Camp of Refuge at Ely.

Conquests secured by the erection of the Tower of London and castles at Exeter, York, Chester.

F. **1072.** William invaded Scotland. Malcolm Canmore paid homage. Submission to William of Edgar Atheling.

William had no more trouble with the English, who soon became his strong supporters through fear of the Norman barons. This alliance between King and people protected English liberty by checking the dangerous power of the barons.

References :
A. "The Harrying of the North." Freeman's *Norman Conquest*, Vol. IV, pp. 287–95.
C. *Hereward the Wake*, by Kingsley, Macmillan.

THE EFFECTS
OF THE NORMAN CONQUEST

I. **England was United under one strong Ruler.**

"It was through community of suffering that the English race learned unity."

A. Lack of union under later Saxon kings.

1. The Danish invasions led to the development of the local power of great nobles for the defence of their own locality.

2. Continuance of mutual jealousy between Wessex, Northumbria, and Mercia. This was aggravated by the growth of the local power of the ealdormen and by Canute's earldoms, and appeared as a factor in the opposition to Godwin in 1051, and in the failure of the Northumbrians and Mercians to help Harold at Hastings.

3. The tendency to disunion increased by the feebleness of later kings of the line of Cerdic, and by the moral decline of the people. Probable seeds of decline even under Edgar. Ethelred the Unready and Edward the Confessor were types of a worn-out stock.

B. The Norman kings were very powerful and able to ensure obedience throughout the country. The power of the Norman kings helped the cause of English liberty by checking the power of the barons at a time when the people were too weak to assert their own rights. Their power due :—

1. To their position as supreme rulers and universal landlords.
2. To the development of a centralised system of government depending upon the King.
3. To the limitation of the power of the barons.
4. To the support of the English after 1072, and of the Church.
5. To the absence of united, national resistance.

C. England was thus saved from the disunion which continued in Germany until the nineteenth century, but the union of England, owing to the later combination of people and nobles, did not lead to despotic monarchy as in France.

II. **The Development and Organisation of the Feudal System.**

A. Anglo-Saxon Feudalism.

Due mainly to the practice of "commendation," by which small landowners surrendered their land to great nobles (Thegns) in return for protection from the Danes, receiving the land back as tenants. The Thegns exercised judicial power in the manorial courts ; but, although the manorial courts sometimes usurped the powers of the local courts, the Anglo-Saxon system was economic rather than political, and land was held, not by military service, but by " customary " regulations. The authority of the Thegns was limited by the facts that

1. The King was the source of all justice.
2. The free shire and hundred courts continued, and were open to all.

3. All Englishmen, whether holding of a Thegn or not, owed allegiance to the King.

But the four earldoms established by King Canute in 1017 gave to their holders far greater power than that of the Thegns, and might have led to a feudal system like that of France if they had lasted long.

B. Feudalism in France.

In France feudalism tended to prevent national unity, and the great nobles, such as the Dukes of Normandy, retained sovereign rights. They exercised supreme judicial authority, exacted an oath of allegiance from all their freemen (who were thus compelled to support their feudal lord against his and their suzerain, the King of France, in case of war), made war, concluded foreign alliances, and issued their own coinage. In Normandy feudalism supplied the machinery of government, and formed the bond of connection between the Duke and his people. The early French kings, although, like the kings of England, they were in theory the suzerains of all their subjects, failed to make that suzerainty a reality.

C. William I and the feudal system in England.

(1) General arrangement.

α. William retained the Anglo-Saxon manorial system.

β. But added a new element by making feudalism a system of land tenure as well as an economic system. The whole country was bound together by the tie of land tenure. The King owned all the land and all men

1. Held their land as tenants of the King.

2. Were bound to serve the King in war in return for the land they held.

γ. The condition of land tenure affected other public work, e.g. the members of the Curia Regis attended, "not because they were great men of Church and State, but because they had entered into a private obligation with the King to attend when called upon as a return for the lands he had given them."

δ. William did not use the feudal system to govern the country. The earldormen were superseded, and the government was entrusted more and more to the royal servants.

(2) The division of the land.

a. All land was held immediately or mediately of the King, who made grants of lands to his Norman followers. The lands of Harold's supporters (Wessex and East Anglia) were confiscated and divided first, on the ground of their treason in opposing the rightful king. The English who accepted William's rule "redeemed" their lands, i.e. received them back from the King on payment of a relief.

Large grants were made not only to the Palatine earls and bishops (Chester, Shrewsbury, Durham, and Kent), who needed large forces to protect the frontiers, but to others (e.g. Cornwall was given to Robert of Mortain, William's cousin). But the danger of combination between the barons was lessened by the grant of holdings in different parts of the country (e.g. Robert of Mortain received also a large grant in the North Riding). This was probably due not to definite policy, but to the gradual conquest of the country.

β. The feudal system completed by the further grant of land to sub-tenants by tenants-in-chief.

England was divided into about 60,000 knights' fees, each worth about £20 per annum, and liable to supply one fully armed knight to serve the King for forty days in each year. This account is based on a statement of Ordericus Vitalis, but Mr. Round (whose theory is now generally accepted) disputes its accuracy. He contends that the Conqueror enfeoffed his tenants-in-chief by a verbal agreement, and on a personal basis and not on a territorial basis of knight service. The estate of the tenant-in-chief had to supply a certain number of knights to serve the King, but he could hire these knights for a money payment or pay them by grants of land as he pleased. Thus every knight did not necessarily hold a knight's fee, although every knight owed service directly to the King.

γ. In addition to military service, money payments had to be made by the grantee to the grantor of land at irregular intervals, but the King, as owner of the body and land of every tenant, had a prior claim on these " Feudal Incidents " if he cared to exercise it. These " Feudal Incidents "[1] included

1. Three " Aids " payable to ransom the lord's person from captivity, on the marriage of his eldest daughter, and the knighting of his eldest son.

2. Reliefs, or succession duties.

3. Wardship. The lord's right of guardianship over a tenant during minority, and of receiving the income of his ward's estate.

4. Marriage. The lord's right of giving a ward in marriage and of receiving a payment from the suitor, or compensation from a ward refusing to marry the suitor proposed by the lord.

5. Escheat. The resumption of the estate by the lord on failure of heirs or felony.

---

[1] These feudal incidents continued long after the feudal system had decayed, and, particularly wardship and marriage, proved most burdensome. They were finally abolished in 1660 at the accession of Charles II, who received instead tonnage and poundage for life and £100,000 per annum.

(3) Checks on the feudal system.

William limited the power of the great barons and thus prevented the tendency to disunion, which was one of the chief results of the system in France.

α. The government was centralised, and officials of the Curia Regis carried out the judicial and financial policy of the King.

β. The earls created by William were not a revival of the powerful earls of Canute, even in the case of the great Palatine earls. The term "earl" tended to become a mark of rank, and no longer implied government of provinces.

γ. The hundred and shire courts were continued, and limited the local power of the barons.

δ. The local administration of the shires was entrusted to the sheriffs, who were the King's agents, and the rebellion of Roger FitzOsbern and Ralph de Guader in 1074 was partly due to the encroachment of the sheriffs in manorial courts.

ε. Owing to the apparent danger of an attack from Saint Canute of Denmark (which soon passed away) William determined to examine his resources. Sworn juries from each hundred and township (the priest, reeve and six villeins) informed the King's commissioners as to the services due to the King. Particulars were furnished as to ownership, extent, population, amount of forest and meadow, number of mills, 1085-6. and value of every manor. This was entered in the Domesday Book,[1] which was an assessment of property for taxation.

[1] The name Domesday was taken either from Domus Dei, a chapel at Winchester, or from the permanence of the record, which was supposed to last until the Day of Doom.

ζ. The King was strongly supported by the English (the old Saxon fyrd was kept up) and by the Church.

η. **1086.** All landholders did homage to the King on Salisbury Plain, and thus the obligation of the sub-tenants to support the King was emphasised.

III. Effect on the Church.

A. The English Church was brought into closer connection with Rome. The Anglo-Saxon Church had been unlearned, isolated. Stigand was deposed and Lanfranc of Pavia, Abbot of Caen, made Archbishop of Canterbury. Lanfranc was a practical statesman and lawyer rather than a great theologian. He thought that the reformation of the Church depended on the maintenance of the power of the Norman kings and worked harmoniously with William I [Lanfranc " William's only friend "] and William II.

B. The English Church was reformed and reorganised.

1. The authority of Canterbury over York was recognised.

2. The Church was strengthened by the national synods frequently held for ecclesiastical legislation (the beginning of legislative independence) and the removal of spiritual pleas from temporal courts (the beginning of judicial freedom).

3. The removal of bishops' sees from small towns and villages to larger towns, e.g. Dorchester (Oxfordshire) to Lincoln.

4. Strong opposition to simony[1] and marriage of the clergy. Reformation of cathedral chapters and great improvement in the character of the clergy.

[1] The purchase of livings, so called from Simon Magus, Acts VIII. 20.

C. But, in spite of the closer connection with Rome, William refused to take the oath of fealty to Pope Hildebrand (Gregory VII), although he sanctioned the payment of Peter's Pence. The King's consent was declared necessary for

1. The recognition of the Pope in England.
2. The meeting of synods.
3. The receipt of Papal bulls.
4. The excommunication of tenants-in-chief.

D. This settlement worked well during Lanfranc's lifetime, but it left undefined the relations between the King and archbishops and bishops and separated Church and lay courts. The former led to the dispute about investiture between Anselm and Henry I, and the latter to the quarrel between Henry II and Becket.

IV. **England Brought into Closer Connection with Western Europe.**

A. The acquisition of Normandy led to ceaseless struggles with France. The French kings always helped English rebels, and the danger from France led to the growth of the English naval power, especially in the Cinque Ports.

B. The connection with Normandy and France and the admission to England of Jewish financiers by William led to an increase in commerce. Skilled craftsmen came from the Continent, especially builders and workers in glass and metal.

C. The tendency to connection with Scandinavia, seen in Canute's time, ceased. Failure of attempts of Sweyn (1069) and Saint Canute (1084) to conquer England.

V. **The Effect on Anglo-Saxon Institutions.**

A. Many old institutions were retained with little change in form; e.g. the Witenagemot became the Magnum Concilium, the manorial system, the hundred and shire courts, and the fyrd were retained.

New institutions included trial by combat and inquests, i.e. investigation by sworn jurors.

B. The growth of the King's power led to greater centralisation and improvement in administration. This was shown by the closer connection between local and central courts which resulted from the itinerant justices sent out by Henry I, under whom the Curia Regis was thoroughly organised.

C. But, although the Normans made comparatively few changes in the old institutions, their genius for organisation and administration infused new life and vigour into them, just as the infusion of Norman blood revived and invigorated the somewhat enfeebled Anglo-Saxon race.

VI. **The Introduction of Norman-French,** a Latin language, which materially affected English, owing to its small number of inflections and the introduction of a new Latin element, including words relating to war, chivalry, law and government. English words relating to common objects and the navy are usually Anglo-Saxon, which has furnished the bulk of our vocabulary. The development of English, owing to the fusion of Norman-French and Anglo-Saxon, was a slow process, and for some time French was spoken by the upper classes, Saxon by the lower, and Latin was the official language.

VII. **The Norman Conquest led to an improvement in Learning, Art, and Civilisation.**

A. The Norman clergy were more learned than the Saxon and new schools were founded.

B. The Norman style of architecture replaced the ruder Saxon work, e.g. The Tower of London and Durham Cathedral.

C. The manners of the Normans were far more refined than those of the Saxons.

References :

A. Feudalism. *Political History of England, 1066–1216,* by Adams, pp. 13–22. Longmans.

Church. Stubbs' *Constitutional History,* Vol. I, pp. 304–12.

Architecture. *An Introduction to the Study of Gothic Architecture,* by J. H. Parker. Parker, chap. III.

WILLIAM I
AND THE NORMAN BARONS

The defeat of Hereward, 1071, and the submission of Malcolm Canmore, 1072, put an end to the resistance of the Saxons. William had then to face the opposition of the discontented Norman Barons.

I. **The Bridal of Norwich, 1075.** (So called because the rising was planned at the wedding of Ralph de Guader to Roger FitzOsbern's sister.)

> Ralph de Guader Earl of Norfolk, Roger FitzOsbern Earl of Hereford, and Waltheof wished to divide England into three feudal duchies: Wessex, Mercia, and Northumbria.   The rising due

A. Mainly to resentment at the checks on the feudal system (page 50), which prevented the barons from getting as much power as the great dukes in France ;

B. Also to the encroachments of the sheriffs in the baronial courts ;

C. And to objection to William's illegitimate birth.

> An attempt was made to secure help from Denmark. Waltheof took a small part in the conspiracy and revealed it to Lanfranc, but was unjustly executed by William, who seized the opportunity of getting rid of the last great Englishman.   The rebellion was put down in the King's absence by Wulfstan, Bishop of Worcester (a Saxon), the Justiciars, and a mixed army of English and Normans.   The beginning of the alliance between the English, fearing the growth of baronial power, and the Norman kings against the barons.

II. **The Rebellion of Robert Curthose, 1078.**

> Robert, a weak and selfish, though popular prince, demanded the Duchy of Normandy, and on his father's refusal attacked Normandy from the castle of Gerberoi,

given him by Philip of France. (The first of many occasions when the King of France helped the rebellious subjects of the King of England.) He was helped by Robert of Belesme and Robert Mowbray, sons of William I's trusted ministers, but submitted after unhorsing his father at the siege of Gerberoi, **1079**.

III. Odo of Bayeux, 1082.

He had received the Earldom of Hereford, **1075**, in addition to his Earldom of Kent, and wished to become Pope. William, considering that Odo's power was dangerous, imprisoned him " not as Bishop of Bayeux, but as Earl of Kent."

Reference :

C. *The Siege of Norwich Castle*, by Blake, Seeley.

WILLIAM I

A. A man of inflexible will and determination (e.g. his march into North Wales 1071) ; stern and merciless in the enforcement of law, " stark man he was and great awe men had of him " (e.g. the Harrying of the North 1069) ; patient (e.g. delayed attacking London after Hastings, and by delay gained more than he would have gained by immediate attack) ; clear-headed and practical, saw what was possible (e.g. pardoned Waltheof when he first revolted, but executed him in 1076).

B. A man of strong religious feeling (although he refused Hildebrand's demand of homage), did not make the Church a source of personal gain, and " in choosing abbots and bishops he considered not so much men's riches or power as their holiness and wisdom." His private life was pure at a time when purity was a rare virtue in kings.

C. A great general. In early youth he defeated the rebellious
barons of Normandy and King Henry I of France. His
skilful manœuvres and personal prowess won the battle
of Hastings, and his subsequent operations were carried
out with skill, rapidity, and success.

D. In some respects was in advance of his age.

    1. He admitted the Jews to England.

    2. Checked the trade in slaves carried on with Ireland by
Bristol merchants.

E. His character deteriorated in his later years. He became
cruel and avaricious. The great blots on his character were

    1069. 1. The ruthless Harrying of the North.

    1076. 2. The unjust execution of Waltheof, who was
less guilty than others who were not executed.

    1071–1080. 3. The making of the New Forest not so bad.

        a. Geology and the history of agriculture show that
this portion of Hampshire was very thinly
populated, and Domesday Book shows that
some part was still inhabited in **1086.**

        β. The popular estimate of this act was due to
hatred of his Forest Laws, to the destruction
of churches within the forest boundary, and
to the tragic deaths in the forest of his sons
Richard and William II, generally supposed to
be a punishment from Heaven for making the
forest.

        γ. William was a mighty hunter, " he loved the tall
deer as if he were their father," and his harsh
Forest Laws (prescribing the loss of eyes for
killing a deer and mutilation for other offences)
caused much suffering.

F. He tried to rule as an English King.

    1. His love of legality led him to accept election by the
Witan and to follow the Anglo-Saxon ritual at his
coronation,

2. His conservatism led him to keep many of the old Anglo-Saxon institutions.

3. He won the support of the English, whom he protected from baronial oppression, and he tried to learn the English language.

4. As a result of his policy England gained unity and freedom long before France and Germany.

References :

A. Freeman's *Norman Conquest*, Vol. II, chap. VIII, p. 1.

B. *Short History of the English People*, pp. 74–6.

WILLIAM II
AND THE NORMAN BARONS

I. The Insurrection of 1088.

William I had left England to Rufus and Normandy to Robert. The barons who held land in both countries feared that the division of rule would prove dangerous to their interests, and nearly all joined a conspiracy formed by Odo of Bayeux to make Robert King of England. They thought that he would prove " more tractable " and that under him they would gain greater power.

The insurrection was easily suppressed owing to the strong support given to William II by the bishops, the Church, and especially by the English led by Wulfstan, Bishop of Worcester.

Odo was captured at Rochester by the English fyrd and exiled. (William later made peace with Robert by the Treaty of Caen, **1091**, by which it was agreed that the survivor should hold England and Normandy, and in **1096** Robert mortgaged Normandy to William for six thousand pounds and went on the First Crusade.)

II. The Insurrection of 1095.

Due to the exactions of Ranulf Flambard, a Norman priest of low birth, who had shown his ability as a royal official, probably in connection with the compilation of Domesday Book, became Justiciar in 1094, Bishop of Durham in 1099, and directed the judicial and financial system. He rigidly maintained the King's feudal rights, and by heavy exactions, especially in the case of reliefs, wardship, and marriage, enriched the King and enraged the barons.

Robert Mowbray, Earl of Northumberland, was the leader of the rising, which was easily put down by the capture of his castle, Bamborough.

III. The Failure of these Insurrections shows

A. The great power of the Norman King, who easily suppressed both risings.

B. The importance of the support given by the English to the King. This was continued in spite of the extortions of Ranulf Flambard, who "drave the gemots," i.e. used the local courts as instruments of extortion, perverted justice, and in 1094 took from the fyrd gathered at Hastings the money contributed by the counties for its maintenance.

WILLIAM II AND THE CHURCH

I. Lanfranc (died 1089).

Steadily supported monarchical power and accepted William's idea that the Church was to be a national Church under his supreme control.

II. Ranulf Flambard.

Strictly applied feudal principles to ecclesiastical as well as to lay fiefs, and insisted on the King's "regalian rights." The King therefore seized vacant sees and took the revenues (e.g. the see of Canterbury was kept vacant for four years after the death of Lanfranc), granted Church lands to his knights, and demanded money payments, analogous to reliefs, from newly appointed bishops.

III. Anselm.

Abbot of Bec, a great theological scholar, was appointed, against his will, to the Archbishopric of Canterbury on the serious illness of William II, 1093. He was quite unable to work with the King as Lanfranc had worked, and compared himself to "an old and feeble sheep yoked to an untamed bull."

A. There was no question of the King's right to appoint Anselm, who acknowledged his feudal obligations.

B. The quarrel between Anselm and William as to the recognition in England of the orthodox Pope Urban II, was an ecclesiastical question. Anselm was technically wrong because no Pope could be recognised in England without the King's consent, but he was successful, and ensured the recognition of Urban II.

C. William summoned Anselm to appear in court for his failure to supply a proper feudal force for the Welsh wars. Anselm refused to appear and was rightly condemned for violating his feudal obligations.

D. The quarrel between the King and Anselm showed

   a. That the settlement made at the Conquest, whereby a bishop was also a feudal baron, was unworkable when the Archbishop and the King did not work together.

   β. That successful opposition to the King was possible.

E. 1097. Anselm exiled.

References:

A. *The Political History of England, 1066–1216*, pp. 93–8.

B. Stubbs' *Constitutional History*, Vol. I, pp. 326–8.

C. *In the Days of St. Anselm*, by Hollis, S.P.C.K

THE CRUSADES

I. Events leading to the Crusades.

A. The religious revival of the tenth century, due mainly to the teaching of the monks of Clugny, but influenced by a belief that the world would come to an end in the year 1000 or in the year 1033, the anniversary of Christ's death. A great increase in pilgrimages to Jerusalem and growth of reverence for the Holy City.

B. **1076.** Capture of Jerusalem by the Seljuk Turks and ill-treatment of Christian pilgrims.

C. **1095.** Europe was roused by the preaching of Peter the Hermit, and a sermon of Pope Urban II at the Council of Clermont led to the First Crusade.

"Never, perhaps, did a single speech of man work such extraordinary and lasting results."—Milman.

D. **1000** (about). The conversion of Hungary to Christianity under King Stephen afforded an overland route to the East, and the Greek Emperors, fearing Turkish attacks, allowed the early Crusaders to pass through Constantinople.

II. The Crusades.

A. **1096.** The First Crusade, led by Godfrey de Bouillon, Raymond of Toulouse, and Robert of Normandy, resulted in the capture of Jerusalem 1099 and the coronation of Godfrey as first King of the Christian kingdom of Jerusalem, which was organised on strict feudal principles.

The object of subsequent crusades was to protect the kingdom of Jerusalem from the Turks.

B. **1147.** Utter failure of the Second Crusade, led by Louis VII of France (first husband of Eleanor of Aquitaine) and the Emperor Conrad III to recover the county of Edessa from the Turks.

C. **1187.** The capture of Jerusalem by Saladin led to the Third Crusade. See page 98.

D. **1204**. Constantinople captured by the soldiers of the Fourth Crusade, who made Baldwin of Flanders first Emperor of the Latin Empire of Constantinople, which lasted until **1261**.

E. **1248–54**. The Sixth Crusade led by St. Louis (Louis IX) of France. Defeat and capture of Louis in Egypt. Pilgrimage of Louis to Palestine.

F. **1291**. Capture of Acre by the Turks and end of the Latin kingdom of Jerusalem.

III. **Results of the Crusades.**

In spite of their failure to wrest Palestine from the Turks the Crusades contributed greatly to the cause of progress in Europe. "It is not too much to say that they have affected, and still remotely do affect, almost every political and social question."—Stubbs.

A. Political.

(1) They saved Eastern Europe from Turkish rule for 450 years. Constantinople, in imminent danger from the Turks in **1096**, was not captured until **1453**.

(2) The enmity between Western, or Roman Catholic, and Eastern Europe adhering to the Greek Church was greatly aggravated by the capture of Constantinople **1204**, and thus the ultimate victory of the Turks was rendered easier.

(3) The absence of many turbulent barons tended to increase the royal power.

B. Religious.

(1) The power of the Pope, under whose auspices the Crusades were undertaken, was strengthened.

(2) Increase in the wealth of the clergy, who readily advanced money to crusading barons on security of their estates. The wealth of the clergy became a cause of much discontent in the fourteenth and fifteenth centuries and was one cause of the Reformation.

C. Chivalry.

> The idea of knighthood passed into that of chivalry when knights fought in the Crusades with the approval of the Church. The duty of protecting the weak and respecting women was now made incumbent on the knight, and chivalry became a refining and ennobling influence.

D. Commercial.

    (1) Great increase of trade not only with Palestine and Egypt, but with Persia and India.

    (2) Development of naval power, especially of Venice, Pisa, and Genoa, owing to the demand for transports. The "Laws of Oleron," issued by Richard I, long remained the maritime code of Western Europe.

E. Learning.

    (1) Europe gained a knowledge of science, especially mathematics and medicine, in which the Arabs had attained great proficiency.

    (2) Geography, Natural History, and Botany were much improved.

    (3) The Crusades supplied worthy material for the historian and William of Tyre was the first historian of the Middle Ages as distinct from a mere writer of chronicles.

    (4) The deeds of the heroes of the Crusades stimulated poets and led to the development of romance.

    (5) The predominance of the French and Normans in the Crusades made French the most general language of Europe for several centuries.

References :

A. Story of the Nations. *The Crusades*, chap. XXVIII.

B. "Capture of Jerusalem." Milman's *Latin Christianity* Vol. IV, p. 188.

C. *God Wills It*, Davis, Macmillan.

THE ACCESSION OF HENRY I, 1100

I. His Claim to the Throne.

He claimed the throne because he was born in England while his father was actually King; he secured it because of Robert's absence in Palestine, his own speed in seizing the castle and royal treasury at Winchester, the loyal support of a few friends led by Henry Earl of Warwick, and his election by some of the leading nobles and clergy.

II. His Charter of Liberties.

A. Clauses :

1. The Church to be free from unjust exactions.
2. The barons to be relieved from unjust reliefs and the abuse of wardship and marriage.
3. The barons to treat the sub-tenants as the King treated them.
4. The laws of King Edward the Confessor to be restored.
5. The King to keep the royal forests.

B. These clauses were not all kept by Henry, but the Charter was important as the foundation of Magna Charta, as a covenant between King and people and a limitation of the royal power.

III. His Marriage.

He married Edith (subsequently called Maud or Matilda), daughter of Margaret and Malcolm Canmore and niece of Edgar Atheling. Thus strengthened his hold on the English, already won over by the Charter.

IV. Anselm Recalled and Restored to Canterbury.

V. Ranulf Flambard Imprisoned.

References :
  A. Stubbs' *Constitutional History*, Vol. I, pp. 328–31.
  B. Freeman's *Norman Conquest*, chap. XXIII, p. 2.

HENRY I AND THE CHURCH

England was now profoundly affected by the work of Pope Hildebrand (1073–1085), who aimed at founding a spiritual autocracy with the Pope at its head ruling all men through the clergy. This implied the reform of the Church, the freedom of the Church from lay interference, and the assertion of Papal supremacy over national churches. The Hildebrandine ideal was accepted by Anselm during his exile.

I. **Church Reform.**

> **1102.** The Synod of Westminster maintained the necessity of clerical celibacy and denounced simony. Anselm thus tried to enforce the neglected canons of Lanfranc.

II. **Investiture.**

> There was as yet no Papal party in England, but the Church, owing to the spread of the ideas of Hildebrand, was becoming conscious of its power. Anselm believed that the cause of the Church was the cause of God, and followed the example of the Papacy by

A. Refusing to do homage to Henry I for his fief, although he had done homage to William II ;

B. Opposing Henry's claim to elect and invest bishops with the ring (the sign that the bishop was wedded to his diocese) and the staff (the emblem of spiritual authority), i.e. by denying the King's right of investiture.

> **1.** The King maintained that, as the State was feudal and the bishops held land, they were under the same obligations to the King as other feudal barons, who were appointed by him and owed him homage. He asserted that William I and William II had exercised full authority over English bishops.

> **2.** Anselm maintained that the bishops, being spiritual, were superior to temporal monarchs, and should be chosen by the Church with regard to spiritual questions alone.
>
> The positions were diametrically opposed and both arguments were logically sound.

1107. 3. The settlement:

    a. The bishops to be elected in the King's courts, to pay homage for their lands to him after election, and then to be invested with the ring and crozier by the Church.

    β. The King gave up the claim to invest bishops with the ring and crozier. Thus Henry gave up the " barren ceremony " of investiture, but retained the control of elections.

        The Church kept the right of investiture and had successfully resisted the attempt of an absolute King to apply the strict interpretation of feudal doctrines to the clergy.

III. Papal Supremacy.

    The belief in the supremacy of the Pope over the Church in England grew owing to the development of the idea of the Church as a world-wide unity dependent on the Pope.

    Henry strenuously asserted the supremacy of the King, and royal consent was still necessary for appeals to Rome and the admission of Papal Legates.

    But the claims of the Papacy were strengthened by the appointment of the Archbishop of Canterbury as a Papal Legate, by the freedom of the Archbishopric of York from the supremacy of Canterbury, by the spread of the Canon Law in England, and by the admission into England about 1130 of the Cistercian monks, who regarded the Pope and not the King as their supreme head.

    Thus, while Henry, owing to his personal power and the support of loyal ministers, maintained his own authority, the Church was gradually gaining ground.

References :

    A. Hildebrand. Milman's *History of Latin Christianity*, Vol. IV, pp. 12–20

HENRY I, THE BARONS, AND NORMANDY

I. **Rebellion in England.**

A. **1101.** The barons led by Robert of Belesme, wishing to keep their estates in England and Normandy, fearing Henry's strong rule and despising Henry as an Englishman and the husband of an English wife, supported Robert of Normandy, who claimed the throne, but peace was made, and Robert withdrew to Normandy, giving up his claim to England in return for 3000 marks a year.

B. **1102.** Defeat of Robert of Belesme by Henry and the English fyrd and capture of Shrewsbury and Bridgenorth castles. Expulsion of Robert and of William of Mortain, Earl of Cornwall. End of rebellion in England. Henceforth "no man in England dared to rebel or hold any castle against him" (Henry I).

II. **Rebellion in Normandy.**

A. Robert Curthose (of Normandy).

Henry was compelled to attack Normandy owing to the danger of a Norman invasion of England by Robert, influenced by Robert of Belesme.

1106. Robert routed at Tinchebrai, which made Normandy subject to England and "reversed the verdict of Senlac." The victory was gained by an English army. Robert was captured and imprisoned in Cardiff Castle until his death.

B. Danger from Louis VI, Louis le Gros, who succeeded Philip I in **1108.** Louis adopted a definite policy of aggrandisement especially against England and Normandy, and was ready to help the opponents of Henry, particularly Robert's son, William the Clito. Henry's position was strengthened

1112 (α) By the capture of Robert of Belesme, "incomparable in all forms of evil."

1113 (β) By the conclusion of a treaty with Louis VI at Gisors.

1113 (γ) By the submission of Fulk, Count of Anjou and Maine.

(δ) By the strong support of Stephen of Blois, Henry's nephew, made Count of Mortain and married to Matilda of Boulogne.

1114 (ε) By the marriage of his daughter Matilda to the Holy Roman Emperor Henry V.

1119 (ζ) By the marriage of Henry's son William to the heiress of Maine.

1119 (η) By the complete defeat of Louis VI, Baldwin of Flanders, and William the Clito at Brenville, and the consequent abandonment by Louis of William's cause.

III. The Succession to the Throne.

A. Henry's son William was drowned in the *White Ship*, 1120. Ruin of Henry's plans. William the Clito, the next legitimate male heir to the English throne, was again supported by Louis VI, Fulk of Anjou and some of the Norman barons led by Waleran de Meulan.

B. To check William the Clito,

1121. Henry married Adela of Louvain, hoping for a male heir.

1123. Defeated Waleran de Meulan.

1124. Persuaded Henry V to attack France on the east.

C. The Empress Matilda.

(1) 1125. The Holy Roman Emperor Henry V died, and

(2) 1126. Henry compelled the barons to recognise the widowed Empress Matilda as heiress to the throne of England.

(3) **1128.** Marriage of Matilda to Geoffrey Plantagenet, son of Fulk of Anjou. (Called Plantagenet from a sprig of broom, *planta genista*, he wore in his helmet.)

> *a.* Henry's policy was wise. By this marriage he detached Fulk from William the Clito, who had been made Count of Flanders by Louis.

1128. William the Clito was killed at Alost. His death removed a possible rival to Matilda, and if Henry had lived ten years longer there would have been no dispute about the succession.

> *β.* The marriage most unpopular.
>
> (1) Matilda objected to the marriage with Geoffrey, who was much younger than herself.
>
> (2) The Normans hated the Angevins, with whom they had repeatedly been at war.
>
> (3) The English barons were not consulted.

(4) **1133.** Birth of Matilda's son Henry. Oath of allegiance taken by the barons to Matilda and the young Henry.

(5) **1135.** Attempt of Geoffrey (now Count of Anjou), supported by the Norman barons, to secure Normandy.
1135. Death of Henry, owing to a surfeit of eels.

IV. General Notes.

A. Henry showed great diplomatic skill in his arrangements for the marriages of William the Atheling and Matilda; in his negotiations with Anjou, Blois, and Flanders against Louis VI; in his success in maintaining the union of England and Normandy.

B. The steady support of the English and the absence of rebellion in England after **1102** left Henry free to fight the Norman rebels and to defend Normandy against the aggression of Louis VI.

C. Henry kept down the Norman barons, but did not completely break their power or settle the succession.

HENRY I AND ENGLAND

In England the great feature of Henry's reign was the development of a strong central administration, dependent on the Crown and connected with the local courts by the itinerant justices. This was rendered easier by the absence of internal war after 1102, and greatly checked the power of the barons.

I. **The Central Administration.**

    A. The Curia Regis. A perpetual committee of the Commune Concilium (the successor in Norman times of the Witenagemot) presided over by the King or Justiciar, in which the King's officials took the leading part. The work was very varied.

        1. Judicial.

            a. A court of primary resort, especially in the case of Norman barons too powerful to accept the verdicts of the local courts.

            β. A court of appeal from the lower courts.

        2. Financial. The Curia Regis sitting as a court for the transaction of financial business was called the Exchequer.

            a. It assessed the Royal Revenue.

            β. It collected the Royal Revenue, receiving the Danegeld, the rent of the Royal domains, feudal payments from landholders, and the proceeds of Royal pleas[1] in local courts. These contributions from the shires were collected by the sheriffs and paid into the Exchequer at Easter and Michaelmas.

            γ. It received the fines imposed under the Forest Laws which were rigidly enforced by Henry I.

---

[1] Even before the Norman Conquest certain cases were reserved for the Crown, in spite of grants of local jurisdiction to the magnates. Under Canute these "placita regia" included assault and neglect of military service. After the Conquest their number increased greatly, owing to the growth of the idea of the King as the personal owner and guardian of the country, and included all felonies.

δ. The increase of public business led to the despatch of barons of the Exchequer as itinerant justices dealing with judicial as well as financial questions, and sitting in the shire courts. By this means the Anglo-Saxon local courts were connected with the Norman central administration.

B. The King's ministers.

(1) The Norman feudal offices were retained. They were held by the great nobles and became hereditary.

a. The High Steward became unimportant owing to the rise of the Justiciar.

β. The Constable and Marshal, originally probably military officials, later exercised important judicial powers.[1]

(2) The new ministerial nobility, the King's personal servants, became of more constitutional importance than the feudal officials, but their offices were obtained by nomination or purchase and not by hereditary right. This new nobility, enriched by valuable grants and dependent on the King, formed a counterpoise to the old feudal nobility.

a. The Justiciar, the King's chief minister, in the King's absence acted as regent. The office became very important under Ranulf Flambard. Henry I's great Justiciar was Roger the Poor, a Norman priest, made Chancellor,[2] Bishop of Salisbury, and Justiciar, who organised the Curia Regis and Exchequer.

β. The Chancellor, the "Secretary of State for all Departments," was originally the head of the clerks of the Chapel Royal.

---

[1] "Constable" from *comes stabuli*.
[2] "Chancellor" from "cancelli," the screen behind which the royal clerks worked.

γ. The Treasurer, the keeper of the royal treasure at Winchester, who examined the sheriffs' accounts and kept one of the three "Pipe Rolls" in which the business of the Exchequer was recorded.

δ. The Chamberlain, head of the audit department.

II. **The Local Courts.**

Henry I restored the courts of the shire and hundred to their old importance, partly perhaps as a recognition of the loyal support given to him by the English.

III. **The Growth of Towns**, due to the increase of commerce and the preservation of peace in England.

A. London.

I. William I, by charter, promised his protection, and guaranteed the succession of a son to his father's property.

II. Henry I, by charter, placed London on a level with the counties, allowed it to elect its own sheriff and justiciar, granted exemption from all jurisdiction save that of its own officers, gave freedom from toll in England, and fixed the ferm (the total amount payable to the King) for London and Middlesex at £300 per annum. The charter of great importance.

α. The city was recognised as a unity, but the unity is that of the shire and not of the municipality. London was not yet a municipal corporation, and the burgesses to whom grants were made were regarded as a body of individuals, not as a corporation.

β. The choice of its own officers, freedom from outside jurisdiction, and the fixture of the ferm, protected the citizens from oppression.

B. Other towns, following the example of London, also gained charters, especially the towns of the royal domain.

IV. **Results of Henry's Policy**.

    A. The cost of his wars and of his administration led to "manifold taxes"; the Forest Laws, which he enforced more sternly than any other king, caused great suffering; bad harvests, and the depreciation of the coinage injured trade.

    B. But England profited greatly by his government. He was "The Lion of Justice," and enforced justice between man and man "No man durst misdo against another in his time." "He gave peace for man and deer." He showed great powers of organisation in his settlement of the administration.

    C. His aims were selfish, his great object was the advancement of his own power, but the means by which this was attained (the limitation of the power of the barons) promoted the welfare of his people.

References:

    A. Towns. *Short History of the English People*, pp. 92–5.

    B. Stubbs' *Constitutional History*, Vol. I, pp. 338, 341.

THE POLICY OF THE NORMAN KINGS TOWARDS WALES

I. **William I**.

    A. The Welsh soon perceived the danger of conquest, and, in **1069**, joined with the Scots, Northerners, and Danes in a rising against the Normans.

1070. Chester occupied, the castle built, the neighbourhood possibly ravaged by William.

    B. Foundation of "Marcher"[1] earldoms. Great power given to Hugh, Earl of Chester, Roger of Montgomery, Earl of Shrewsbury (the father of Robert of Belesme), and William Fitz-Osbern, Earl of Hereford. Out of a probable total of six earldoms three were founded on the Welsh border to check the Welsh. Castles built in the earldoms and at Cardiff and Monmouth.

        Wulfstan, the English bishop of Worcester, was faithful and vigilant.

[1] i.e. the earldoms of the "Marches" or borders. Compare Mercia, the border country, and the German "Marks."

C. The establishment of these Marcher earldoms was necessary but dangerous, because these barons became very powerful (e g. Roger of Montgomery rebelled in **1088**, and Robert of Belesme frequently).

II. William II.

A. **1093** (about). The beginning of the policy of "conquest by settlement." Permission was given to the Norman barons to keep lands conquered from the Welsh. This policy proved successful, especially in South Wales, where Fitzhamon, lord of Glamorgan, greatly extended his power.

B. **1094**. General rising of the Welsh against the Marcher barons.

C. **1095** and **1097**. Unsuccessful expeditions of William II to Wales.

D. During this reign the Welsh maintained their independence in the mountains, but a considerable portion of the lowlands was gained by the Normans.

III. Henry I.

A. **1114**. The Welsh were defeated and submitted, but Henry relied on the gradual incorporation of Wales by the barons rather than on conquest by royal armies.

B. He put a Flemish colony in Pembroke, hence called "Little England beyond Wales."

C. He put English bishops into Welsh sees. These reformed the Welsh Church, built monasteries, and ensured the recognition by the Welsh of the supremacy of Canterbury.

D. Cardiganshire was given to Gilbert de Clare.

E. Henry's illegitimate son, Robert of Caen (son of Nesta, a Welsh lady), was created Earl of Gloucester, and gained great estates in South Wales by his marriage with the heiress of Fitzhamon.

IV. Stephen.

Successful revolt in South Wales. Danger of expulsion of Normans and Flemings.

Stephen did not interfere owing to the Civil War in England, and thus risked the loss of Wales.

References :

C. *Pabo the Priest*, by Baring Gould, Methuen.

THE NORMAN KINGS AND SCOTLAND

The Kings of Scotland repeatedly attempted to conquer the North of England, and made the most of opportunities afforded by rebellions and wars in England.

I. **William I.**

A. Malcolm III (Canmore) nominally accepted the Conquest, 1068, but the Scottish court afforded refuge to English exiles. He married Margaret, granddaughter of Edmund Ironside, owing to whose influence

   (1) The Scottish church was brought under the influence of Rome.

   (2) The English language and customs were introduced.

   (3) Commerce grew and civilisation was more widely diffused.

B. Malcolm III's policy was to extend the southern border of his territory to the Tees. Hence arose continual danger of Scottish raids in the North.

1070. He attacked the north on behalf of Edgar Atheling.

1079. He attacked the north when William I was away in Normandy.

II. **William II.**

1091. Malcolm III attacked the north when William II was away in Normandy, but submitted and acknowledged himself the man of Rufus.

1092 William II captured Cumberland, and built a castle at Carlisle to guard the north-west entrance into England. This was a conquest of territory from Scotland and fixed the present boundary between England and Scotland.

1093. Malcolm, owing to the loss of Cumberland, again invaded the north, but was killed at Alnwick. Margaret died at the same time, and the dispute as to the succession in Scotland put an end to the danger of Scottish invasions. Rufus supported the English party and Edgar, son of Malcolm III.

III. **Henry I.**

1100. Henry married Edith (Matilda), daughter of Malcolm III and Margaret, and friendly relations were maintained between England and Scotland in his reign.

IV. **Stephen.**

David, brother of Edith, invaded England to maintain the cause of his niece Matilda against Stephen, and also to extend his territory.

1136. First Invasion : Stephen ceded Cumberland to David.

1138. Second Invasion : David defeated at Northallerton[1] by the northern levies under Thurstan.

1139. Peace made between David and Stephen, who invested David's son Henry with the earldom of Northumberland (except Newcastle and Bamborough), which David claimed through his wife the daughter of Waltheof and granddaughter of Siward Earl of Northumbria.

1149. David, in alliance with Ralph of Chester, invaded England on behalf of Henry, Matilda's son. The expedition failed owing to the desertion of the Earl of Chester. David, however, had succeeded in securing England north of the Eden and the Tees.

THE REIGN OF STEPHEN, 1135-54

1. **The Accession of Stephen, 1135.**

A. Stephen of Blois, son of William I's daughter Adela, had been made Count of Mortain by Henry I, and had married Matilda of Boulogne. Through fear of Angevin rule he was accepted as King by the citizens of London and Winchester. He was crowned by the Archbishop of Canterbury and recognised by the Pope in spite of the oath of allegiance he had sworn to his cousin Matilda.

B. He won over many of the nobles by lavish grants, was accepted by Henry I's "new men" including Robert of

---

[1] The Battle of the Standard. The banners of St. Cuthbert of Durham, St. Wilfred of Ripon, St. Peter of York, and St. John of Beverley were fastened to a car and formed the standard of the English army.

Gloucester, Matilda's half-brother, and Roger Bishop of Salisbury, and issued charters promising freedom of election and jurisdiction to the Church and the abolition of the Forest Laws. His position was therefore due to bargaining and loyal support could hardly be expected for "a King by contract," especially from the turbulent barons who took advantage of his weakness to build many castles and to demand large grants of land and money.

C. Although he successfully crushed a revolt of Hugh Bigod, 1136, and resisted an attack of Geoffrey of Anjou on Normandy, 1135, he lost power owing to his failure to raise up "new men" to check the barons and owing to undue leniency to rebels. His employment of foreign mercenaries, whom he could not properly control, and his resumption of the forests in spite of his promise to give them up, alienated some supporters.

II. Events to 1139.

1136. Stephen ceded Cumberland to David of Scotland, who had invaded England on behalf of Matilda.

1138. David of Scotland routed at Northallerton (Battle of the Standard) by the northern levies summoned by Thurstan, Archbishop of York.

1138. Robert of Gloucester renounced his allegiance at Bristol and fled to Normandy.

1139. David of Scotland was reconciled to Stephen by Queen Matilda of Boulogne. Grant of the Earldom of Northumberland (except Newcastle and Bamborough) to David's son Henry.

III. Stephen's Quarrel with the Church.

A. **1138.** Stephen's brother, Henry Bishop of Winchester, who had supported Stephen's accession, was greatly disappointed because Stephen refused to allow his promotion to the vacant Archbishopric of Canterbury. Henry was soon appointed Papal Legate.

B. 1139. Stephen arrested the Justiciar, Roger Bishop of Salisbury, his son Roger the Chancellor, and his nephew Alexander Bishop of Lincoln nominally for building and fortifying castles. Roger's castle at Devizes was captured and another nephew, Nigel Bishop of Ely, the Treasurer, arrested. The bishops were treated with much indignity.

    a. Stephen's most foolish action was possibly due to fear that Roger's wealth would be used for Matilda or (as in his brother Henry's case **1138**) from a desire to weaken the growing power of the Church.

    β. The result was the immediate alienation of the clergy from Stephen and the utter collapse of the Government.

IV. The Civil War, 1139-53.

A. Normandy.

In spite of Stephen's success in **1137** Normandy was gradually conquered by Geoffrey of Anjou, who in **1144** received the formal grant of the duchy from the King of France.

B. 1139. The Empress Matilda.

The Empress Matilda and Robert of Gloucester landed in England. The Dowager Queen Adela surrendered Matilda to Stephen, who very foolishly allowed her to join Robert, and thus lost an opportunity of ending the war at once.

1141. Stephen was captured at Lincoln. Matilda was elected Queen in a Council of Clergy at Winchester, through the influence of Bishop Henry, and accepted by London. She soon showed her incapacity for rule by alienating Henry and the Londoners (owing to her refusal to confirm the laws of King Edward the Confessor). Fled from London to Oxford. Henry rejoined his brother Stephen's party. Robert of Gloucester was captured while attacking Winchester and exchanged for Stephen. Stephen besieged Matilda in Oxford. Oxford was captured, but Matilda escaped to Wallingford.

1142–7. The war continued. Matilda was supported by the West, and her brother's town of Bristol was the centre of her power ; London and the East supported Stephen.

1147. Death of Robert of Gloucester.

1148. Matilda returned to Normandy.

C. Henry Plantagenet.

1147–52. A cessation of hostilities except for an invasion of King David and Henry Plantagenet in Lancashire in alliance with Ralph Earl of Chester, 1149. Failure of the expedition owing to the treachery of Ralph.

1150. Geoffrey Plantagenet gave up the Duchy of Normandy to his son Henry.

1151. Henry obtained Anjou, Touraine, and Maine on Geoffrey's death.

1152. Henry married Eleanor of Aquitaine, the divorced wife of Louis VII (Louis le Jeune).

1152. Theobald Archbishop of Canterbury refused to crown Eustace as King during his father Stephen's lifetime.

1153. Henry landed and the war was renewed but soon concluded, on the death of Eustace, by the Treaty of Wallingford, which provided that Henry was to succeed Stephen.

1154. Stephen died.

V. The results of Stephen's Reign.

A. The Barons.

The barons, profiting by the weakness of the King and of Matilda, had secured higher titles and larger estates by bargaining with both. Stephen created nine earls and Matilda six, but these earldoms were only marks of rank and did not, as under Canute, imply an official position, although "the fiscal earls" received grants of money. The power of the barons was increased by the erection of 375 adulterine castles.[1]

[1] Castles built without royal licence.

α. The growth of the power of the barons and the collapse of Henry I's administrative system led to feudal anarchy and showed the grave dangers arising from feudalism if not checked by a strong king. The country people suffered greatly from the oppression of the barons. "They cruelly oppressed the wretched men of the land with castle-works. Never did heathen men do worse than they did. Men said openly that Christ and his saints slept."

β. At one time it seemed likely that independent feudal principalities would be established, especially by Geoffrey de Mandeville Earl of Essex and by Ralph Earl of Chester. This danger was averted by the deaths of Geoffrey and Ralph and by the vigorous action of Henry in destroying adulterine castles and restoring the royal power after the Treaty of Wallingford.

B. The Church.

I. The Church alone gained permanent advantage from Stephen's reign. The clergy, the only united and organised body, legislated and judged their own cases without restraint and exercised most powerful influence in the selection of the monarch in **1135, 1141, 1152,** and **1153.**

II. The acquisition of independent judicial power led to an increase in appeals to Rome.

III. A great monastic revival took place and 115 monasteries all owning obedience to Rome, were built between **1135** and **1154** largely by the Cistercians, who did much to develop commerce and agriculture in the north of England.

IV. Archbishop Theobald was a patron of learning and promoted the study of Civil Law in England.

C. London. The war showed the growing importance of London as a political factor, e.g. in the choice and rejection of Matilda.

D. Stephen left to Henry II the task of re-establishing the royal authority over barons and clergy, and of wresting Northumberland and Cumberland from the Scots.

References :

A. Stubbs' *Constitutional History*, Vol. I, pp. 344–64.

C. *For King or Empress*, by Whistler, Nelson.

THE SETTLEMENT OF ENGLAND

England was exhausted by the civil war, and there was no one strong enough to resist successfully the attempt of Henry, relying upon the forces of Normandy, Aquitaine, Anjou, and of his English supporters, to restore the royal power, the failure of which in the previous reign had brought on England all the evils of the feudal system.

I. The End of Anarchy.

A. Expulsion of Stephen's foreign mercenaries.

B. Resumption of royal castles.

C. Destruction of remaining adulterine castles.

D. Abolition of exchequer pensions paid to the fiscal earls and resumption of most of Stephen's grants. Some earls, e.g. the Earls of Oxford and Essex, confirmed in their possessions as a reward for allegiance to Henry II.

William of Aumale compelled to surrender Scarborough.

Roger of Hereford gave up the castles of Hereford and Gloucester.

1155. Hugh de Mortimer's castle of Bridgenorth captured by the English fyrd. The most serious resistance offered to Henry.

E. Great councils were frequently held, and thus the general support of the baronage was secured against powerful individuals.

F. The coinage was restored.

> The establishment of peace was a great blessing The barons lost the opportunity of playing off one party against another, and the English gladly supported Henry, who promised to restore the conditions of " King Henry my grandfather." The success of the settlement was shown by the fact that there was no rising in England for nearly eighteen years.

II. The Restoration of the Administration.

A. The Curia Regis and Exchequer and judicial circuits were restored.

B. The King showed great wisdom in his choice of ministers. Richard de Lucy and Robert de Beaumont were made Justiciars. Nigel Bishop of Ely, nephew of Roger Bishop of Salisbury, was given charge of the Exchequer, which he successfully reorganised. Thomas Becket made Chancellor 1154.

III. Scotland.

1157. Malcolm IV, successor of David, gave up Northumberland and Cumberland, paid homage and was invested with the earldom of Huntingdon.

IV. Wales.

1157. Submission of Owen Prince of North Wales and Rhys Prince of South Wales.

Reference :

A. Stubbs' *Constitutional History*, Vol. I, pp. 482–93.

HENRY II AND THE CHURCH

Henry's great object of making the royal power supreme involved the extension of that power over the Church, which had gained a considerable measure of independence, especially in jurisdiction, during Stephen's reign.

I. **Thomas Becket, 1118–70.**

    A. Born **1118.** Son of a merchant of London. Well educated, especially in law, and possessed great ability as an administrator and organiser. Trained in the service of Archbishop Theobald. Became very friendly with Henry II, who appointed him Chancellor **1154.** Negotiated a marriage between Henry II's son Henry and Louis VII's daughter in **1158**, and took an active part in the campaign against Toulouse, **1159.** As Chancellor showed great fidelity to the King. His splendid style of living attracted great attention.

    B. **1162.** Appointed Archbishop of Canterbury on Theobald's death.

        I. Resigned the chancellorship and adopted a simpler mode of life.

        II. He accepted Hildebrand's theory of the supremacy of the clergy to all laity, asserted that "the clergy are above kings," denied the right of laymen to judge the clergy, and insisted on the enforcement of all clerical privileges. This position was absolutely inconsistent with the royal supremacy, and a quarrel between Henry and Becket became inevitable.

    C. The quarrel with the King.

    1163. Becket refused to pay a land tax into the Exchequer, thus making it part of the regular royal revenue, instead of to the sheriffs as hitherto. The King gave way.

        1. Becket's quarrel with Henry began on a secular point.

        2. The first case of successful opposition to taxation since the Conquest.

D. The trial of the clergy.

   I. The development of the Canon Law and the Clugniac reformation had led to an increase in the power of the ecclesiastical courts. These had been separated from the lay courts by Lanfranc, had been the only means of obtaining justice during much of Stephen's reign, and in consequence had encroached upon the jurisdiction of the lay courts. But the Church courts could inflict only spiritual penalties, the severest being degradation, and the benefit of clergy (which gave the right of trial in the Church courts) was very widely extended. The Church courts could not inflict adequate punishment, and one hundred murders had been committed by clergymen since Henry's accession. Henry therefore determined to make clergymen amenable to lay courts in order

      a. To bring them under the royal power.

      β. To check crime.

  II. In spite of Becket's opposition the Constitutions of Clarendon were passed 1164.

      a. Clerks accused of crime were to appear first in the King's Court. On conviction to be degraded by the Church courts, and then to be sent to the lay courts for punishment according to the law of the land.

        Becket objected to this, asserting,

          (1) That laymen ought not to judge clergymen.

          (2) That this law inflicted a double punishment for one crime.

      β. The Curia Regis to decide whether a suit between a layman and a clerk should be tried in the Church or lay courts.

      γ. Sons of villeins not to receive holy orders without their lord's consent.

δ. No tenant in chief to be excommunicated without the King's consent.

ε. No bishops to leave the country without the King's consent.

ζ. No appeals to be made to Rome without the King's consent.

η. Bishops to be elected on the King's summons in the King's chapel, and with the King's consent.

θ. The clergy to hold their lands as feudal baronies.

> (1) Henry maintained that he had only reasserted the customs of Henry I, and this was generally true.
>
> (2) But, owing to the policy of Hildebrand, to the work of Anselm, and to the growth of ecclesiastical power in Stephen's reign, the Church had become much stronger than in Henry I's time, and the Constitutions weakened this power and checked clerical pretensions.

E. Later history of Becket.

It is doubtful whether Becket openly refused his assent, but he resolved not to accept the Constitutions.

I. He refused to take the King's pleas in his own court, and disobeyed a summons to appear before the Curia Regis at Northampton, 1164, to answer for this refusal (i.e. he refused attendance at the court of his feudal superior). He was rightly condemned for this by the Curia Regis, which asserted the feudal liabilities of the clergy.

II. The King, wishing to ruin Becket, demanded the accounts of his chancellorship.

III. Becket appealed to Rome in spite of the Constitutions, and asserted dishonestly, "We promised nothing at Clarendon without excepting the rights of the Church."

IV. **1164.** Becket fled to France, and forbade the clergy to obey the Constitutions.

V. **1170.** Nominal reconciliation between Henry and Becket, who suspended the Archbishop of York and excommunicated the Bishops of London and Salisbury for taking part in the coronation of Prince Henry, asserting that the right of crowning the King belonged to the Archbishop of Canterbury. Return of Becket to England. Anger of Henry at the excommunication of the bishops and consequent

VI. Murder of Becket, **1170**, in Canterbury Cathedral, but *not* on the steps of the altar.

The King's position was greatly weakened by the murder of Becket, who was regarded as a martyr and revered as a saint. The King renounced the Constitutions, and so secured absolution from the Pope for the murder for which he was held responsible. The clergy regained the right of appeals to Rome, the Church courts continued to try clergy accused of felony (except treason), and retained jurisdiction over two important civil cases, those relating to marriage and wills.[1] But Henry had asserted the cause of Royal Authority and Common Law, and, although the separation between the lay and ecclesiastical courts continued, he had extended the jurisdiction of the former.

References :

A. Stubbs' *Constitutional History*, Vol. I, pp. 498 – 504. Henry II in *Twelve English Statesmen*, chap. v

B. *Short History of the English People*, p. 108.

[1] Probate and divorce cases are still taken in the same court.

HENRY II AND THE BARONS

The assertion of the royal supremacy involved the weakening of the power of the feudal barons as well as of the clergy.

The Assertion of Royal Authority over the Barons.

A. The barons' power greatly weakened by the strong measures at the beginning of the reign (p. 80).

B. The new regulations regarding military service weakened the barons.

(1) Scutage **1159.** A money payment instead of actual military service [literally "shield money," from Latin *scutum*].

a. In Anglo-Saxon times a warrior who failed to serve paid a fine called "fyrdwite" to the King.

1156. β. Henry II received money from the clergy in lieu of military service for their lands.

1159. γ. Henry II, during his expedition to Toulouse, extended the system to lay tenants, and accepted a payment of two marks in lieu of the service of a knight. Knights who were sub-tenants paid directly to the King and not to their overlord, as their service was due to the King.

Henry thus weakened the dangerous feudal armies, obtained a large sum of money with which he could hire for foreign service a non-baronial army which was not limited to forty days' service, the time for which feudal knights were liable to serve.

(2) The Assize of Arms, **1181,** due partly to the feudal rebellion of **1173.**

A revival of the old Saxon "fyrd" or national levy. Every man to provide himself with arms according to his rank, and to serve in the militia.

Henry thus obtained for home service a non-baronial army composed mainly of English, the steady supporters of the King against the barons.

C. The organisation of the judicial work of the Curia Regis
    (p. 87) weakened the baronial jurisdiction
    α. By admitting the itinerant judges of the Ex-
        chequer to the baronial courts by the Assize of
        Clarendon 1166.
    β. By increasing the importance of the shire courts.
    γ. By the Grand and Petty Assizes (page 88) which
        brought civil cases regarding land under the
        royal jurisdiction.
D. 1170. The Inquest of Sheriffs.
    The sheriffs as representatives of the King were most
important officials, and exercised supreme authority in
the shires. The office was frequently held by feudal
barons, whose power was in consequence greatly increased.
By the Inquest of Sheriffs Henry removed these baronial
sheriffs and replaced them by officials of the Exchequer.
Thus the local power of the barons was weakened.

THE LEGISLATION OF HENRY II

I. The Constitutions of Clarendon, 1164 (pages 83–4).
II. The Organisation and Extension of the Judicial Work of
    the Curia Regis.
A. 1166. The Assize[1] of Clarendon. No franchise to exclude
    the royal justices, i.e. the itinerant judges of the Exchequer
    could sit in baronial as well as in shire and hundred courts.
B. 1176. The Assize of Northampton.
    England divided into six circuits, each with three judges
    of the Exchequer representing the King.
C. 1178. Five judges of the Curia Regis appointed to hear
    appeals. The origin of the Court of King's Bench. An
    appeal allowed from the King's Bench to the King
    sitting in the Commune Concilium.[2]
    The Curia Regis was thus brought into close connec-
    tion with local courts, and suitors received protection
    from baronial oppression.

[1] The word assize means either a law, as in the Assizes of Clarendon, Northampton, and Arms, or an assembly, or a form of trial as in the Grand Assize.
[2] Appeals later were often made to the Privy Council, which is still the
final court of appeal in ecclesiastical and colonial cases.

III. The Development of the Jury System.

The common people, the strong supporters of the King, now took an important part in the administration of justice, and local knowledge was used to ascertain facts in dispute.

The Jury System was introduced into England by the Normans, and used, e.g., in the compilation of the Domesday Book, **1086,** when the priest, reeve, and six villeins gave information about their own township. It was greatly extended by Henry II, and supplied a new method of legal procedure

A. The Jury and Civil Cases.

a. The Grand Assize.

Twelve sworn knights of the locality, "Recognitors," to give evidence in cases of disputed claims to land as an alternative to trial by battle between the claimants. This Grand Assize was the origin of the modern Civil Jury.

β. Petty Assizes.

Twelve men (freeholders were eligible as well as knights) to give evidence in cases of Novel Disseisin, Morte d'Ancestor, Darrein Presentment dealing with unjust dispossession of land, the conditions of the tenure of a deceased ancestor, and the right of presenting the land.

Thus the jurors were originally witnesses to fact rather than judges of fact as at present.

γ. These Assizes led to a great increase of the Royal authority in Civil cases.

B. The Jury and Criminal Cases.

1166. Assize of Clarendon.

Twelve men from each hundred aud four men from each township to present reputed criminals for trial by ordeal before the itinerant justice and the sheriff in the County Court. If the prisoner failed at the ordeal he received the legal punishment of his crime, if successful he was exiled,

> α. Compurgation, by which the evidence as to a
> man's character varied in value according to
> the social position of the witness, was now
> discontinued.
>
> β. This "jury of presentment" was the origin of
> our Grand Jury.

C. The Jury was used for financial purposes, e.g. to assess
personal property (Saladin Tithe), **1188**, and real property (Great Carucage), **1198**.

D. Later history of the Jury.

> α. Ordeal was abolished by the Lateran Council
> **1215**, and a petty jury established to accept or
> refuse presentments made by the Grand Jury.
>
> β. "Afforcing jurors" possessing special knowledge
> of the case were subsequently added to the
> sworn jury.
>
> γ. Separation of "afforcing jurors" from the petty
> jury. The former became witnesses, the latter
> "became judges of the fact, the law being
> declared by the presiding officer acting in the
> King's name."

IV. **The Assize of Arms, 1181** (page 86)

V. **The Assize of the Forest, 1184.**

Earls, barons, knights, freeholders, and all men concerned were ordered to attend the King's forest courts.

Regulations for preservation of game and timber to be
rigidly enforced.

VI. **Results of Henry's Legislation.**

A. Decrease in the importance of feudalism.

> α. The general work of government was to be
> carried out by trained non-feudal officials.
>
> β. The sheriffs became royal officers.
>
> γ. The feudal armies became less important after
> the establishment of scutage and the revival
> of the fyrd by the Assize of Arms.

B. The growth of national Common Law, which had no respect for persons and ignored clerical and baronial privileges and immunities. This law had its source in the King, and was interpreted in the King's Courts by royal justices.

C. The re-establishment of the Norman absolutism based on popular support. But there was a tendency to excessive concentration, and the King's Courts were overburdened.

References :

A. Stubbs' *Constitutional History*, Vol. I, pp. 505–12.

Taswell - Langmead's *English Constitutional History*, pp. 133–41. "The Jury."

HENRY II AND IRELAND

I. Pope Hadrian IV.

Hadrian IV (Nicholas Breakspear, the only English Pope), wishing to strengthen the power of the Pope in Ireland, granted it to Henry II, 1155, in virtue of the ownership of all islands which he claimed for the Papacy.[1]

No expedition was undertaken at the time, owing to the opposition of Henry's mother, the Empress Matilda.

II. The "Conquest of Ireland," 1166–71.

A. 1166. Henry gave permission to Dermot (Diarmid), the exiled King of Leinster, to obtain the assistance of the Norman barons.

Reconquest of Leinster by the soldiers of Robert Fitz-Stephen and Maurice FitzGerald. Their armour, archers, and better weapons gave the Normans, though much inferior in numbers, a great advantage over the unarmoured Irish.

B. 1170. Richard de Clare Earl of Pembroke (Strongbow) went to Ireland, married Eva, the daughter of Dermot, and, on the death of Dermot, succeeded to Leinster.

[1] The so-called Bull Laudabiliter was *not* the instrument by which the grant was made, but probably a student's exercise.

C. 1171. The Assertion of Henry's Authority.

I. Henry, fearing the formation of an independent Norman principality, and anxious to leave England until the resentment at Becket's murder had subsided, went to Ireland.

II. Homage paid by Strongbow for Leinster.

III. General submission to Henry of the Irish chiefs of the South and East. (Not of Roderick, King of Connaught, who claimed authority over all Ireland, nor of the kings of the extreme North-West. The term " Conquest of Ireland " is therefore inaccurate.)

IV. The settlement of Ireland.

    1172. α. At the Council of Cashel the Irish bishops swore allegiance to Henry, and passed canons against the marriage of the clergy.

        β. Dublin, Waterford and Wexford became part of the royal domain.

        γ. Hugh de Lacy was made Justiciar.

        δ. Ireland was regarded as a part of England, not as a separate colony.

V. 1173. Henry returned to England owing to the rebellion of his son Henry, and on his departure disorder again broke out in Ireland.

III. John in Ireland.

Gradual extension of Norman rule in Ireland. Submission of Roderick of Connaught.

1185. Prince John appointed (never crowned) King of Ireland. Alienation of the native princes by John's rudeness. Desertion of many of his soldiers. Return of John and speedy loss of most of Ireland. Henry's possessions confined to the " Pale,"[1] the district around Dublin.

References :

A. " Henry II." *Twelve English Statesmen*, chap. VIII,

[1] *L.*, *palus*, an enclosure.

THE REBELLION
OF THE YOUNG HENRY, 1173-4

I. Causes.

A. Henry II, while allowing his sons considerable power refused to grant them complete independence.

  I. The young Henry, who had been crowned King in 1170, and also (together with his wife Margaret of France) in 1172, demanded either Normandy or England as a separate kingdom.

  II. Richard, appointed governor of Aquitaine and Poitou, and Geoffrey Count of Brittany also desired independence, and were urged to rebel by their mother, Eleanor.

B. For John (nicknamed "Lackland" because no land had as yet been assigned to him), Henry tried to arrange a marriage with the daughter of the Count of Maurienne and promised him part of Anjou. Consequent opposition of

  α. The young Henry, to whom Anjou had been granted.

  β. Louis VII, because the acquisition by John of the county of Maurienne in Burgundy would give him the control of the western passes of the Alps, and would check the extension of France towards the south-east.

C. Louis VII gladly supported the rising which threatened to break up Henry II's dominions, and which might prevent John from getting Maurienne.

D. William the Lion, King of Scotland, supported the young Henry on condition of receiving Northumberland, which Malcolm IV had been compelled to give up to Henry II, 1157.

E. The young Henry promised Kent to the Count of Flanders and Mortain to the Count of Boulogne, who had married King Stephen's daughter.

F. Most of the great Norman barons led by Hugh Bigod, Earl of Norfolk, the Earls of Leicester and Chester, joined the rebels, owing to their resentment at the limitation of their power by Henry (page 80).

II. The rebellion easily suppressed.

Henry II was strongly supported by the newly created baronage, by the English clergy and people, and by the royal officials led by the Justiciar De Lucy.

A. Abroad.

1173. Complete defeat of the Earl of Chester at Dol in Brittany by Henry, assisted by a large force of Flemish mercenaries.

B. In England.

The rebellion crushed without the King's personal interference.

1174. De Lucy routed and captured the Earl of Leicester at Fornham in Norfolk.

1174. Henry II conciliated popular feeling by doing penance for the murder of Becket. William the Lion captured at Alnwick by the northern levies. Defeat of the rebel fleet and submission of Hugh Bigod.

III. Results of the Rebellion.

A. Final overthrow of the feudal power of the Norman barons. Their castles were destroyed, and the barons were never again strong enough to oppose the King by themselves.

B. **1174.** The Treaty of Falaise. William the Lion paid homage to Henry II for Scotland, and English garrisons occupied the chief Scottish castles.

The fidelity of the English was the main cause of Henry's success.

References :

A. " Henry II." *Twelve English Statesmen,* chap. IX.

HENRY II's FOREIGN POLICY

Henry's vast Continental possessions (page 96) made his foreign policy as important as his administrative work in England. His aim was the consolidation rather than the extension of his dominions.

I. France.

Henry's relations with France were the most important part of his foreign policy.

Henry's possessions in France were far greater than those of the King, and formed the chief obstacle to the extension of the royal domain, the chief factor in the history of France during the early Middle Ages.

A. Louis VII.

In spite of efforts to make peace between England and France (e.g. by the marriage of the young Henry and Louis' daughter Margaret), there were frequent wars between Henry II and Louis VII, who made the most of opportunities afforded by the quarrels of Henry and his sons.

(1) Henry made some attempt to extend his dominions in France, but his efforts were generally directed to the preservation of peace and the maintenance of good government in his territory.

1158. Henry obtained the county of Nantes, thus commanding the mouth of the Loire and gaining a point of attack on Brittany.

1159. Failure of his attempt to capture Toulouse, which was claimed by his wife Eleanor.

Henry became suzerain of Brittany owing to the marriage of his son Geoffrey with the heiress.

1173. Failure to secure Maurienne for John.

(2) **1173.** Strong support given by Louis VII to his son-in-law, the young Henry, whose demand for a separate kingdom tended greatly to weaken the Angevin Empire.

B. Philip Augustus, **1180.**

(1) Philip Augustus succeeded his father, Louis VII, in **1180.** At first his relations with Henry II were friendly, and Henry reconciled Philip with his powerful uncles, the Counts of Blois and Champagne, who resented the influence exercised over the young King by Count Philip of Flanders, the uncle of the Queen.

(2) But Philip soon saw the need of weakening Henry's power in France, while Henry failed to appreciate the danger from the bold and unscrupulous Philip, who negotiated with Henry's disloyal sons.

1183. On the death of the young Henry, Philip demanded the return of the Vexin (the dowry of his widowed sister Margaret), which afforded an entrance into Normandy on the south-east.

1186. Death of Geoffrey of Brittany in the midst of negotiations with Philip against his father. Demand by Philip of the wardship of Geoffrey's heiress.[1]

1188. Henry foolishly refused to recognise Richard of Aquitaine as his heir. Alliance of Richard and Philip, afterwards joined by John, against Henry.

1189. The allies captured Le Mans, and Henry was compelled—

    a. To accept Richard as his successor,

    β. To acknowledge Philip's suzerainty over his French possessions.

1189. Death of Henry at Chinon. His last words, "Shame on a conquered King."

---

[1] Arthur of Brittany was born after his father's death.

II. **The Marriages of Henry's Daughters**.

    a. Henry's daughter Eleanor married Alfonso VIII of Castile.

    β. Henry's daughter Matilda married Henry the Lion, Duke of Saxony, the head of the family of the Guelphs, and thus became the ancestress of King George V.

    γ. Henry's daughter Joanna married William the Good, the Norman King of Sicily.

        Henry's influence in Europe was greatly strengthened by these marriages. His importance shown

            (1) By his selection as arbitrator of a dispute between Castile and Navarre,

            (2) By the offer of the crown of Jerusalem **1185**.

III. **His suzerainty recognised in North and South Wales** (p. 81), **Scotland** (p. 93), **and part of Ireland** (p. 91).

IV. **General Criticism**.

    Henry in his foreign politics attempted an impossible task. His empire was too divided to make permanent union possible. The possession of land in France made lasting hostility between England and France inevitable, and the tradition of friendship between England and Spain, North Germany and Sicily, which Henry founded, by no means compensated for this hostility.

KING HENRY II

I. **Henry was one of the richest Princes in Christendom**.

    A. He got Normandy from his mother, obtaining the duchy (conquered and handed over to him by his father Geoffrey) in **1150**. Louis VII tried to conquer it **1151**, but failed. Louis VII recognised Henry as Duke of Normandy.

    B. He got Anjou, Maine, and Touraine on the death of his father **1151**.

C. He married Eleanor of Aquitaine, the divorced wife of Louis VII, 1152, and thus got Aquitaine, Poitou, Perigord, Quercy, Limousin, Gascony, and claims on Toulouse. Louis was at once reduced to the scanty territories of the Capetian House and rivalry between France and England was ensured for 300 years.

D. King of England, claimed through his mother, 1154.

E. He ruled most of South Wales and exercised feudal rights over North Wales.

F. Suzerain of Scotland after 1174.

He was thus lord of Western Europe from Scotland to the Pyrenees.

BUT α. The bond of union was personal, viz. subjection to one king, not subjection to England, nor community of race or language. The Angevin Empire was an empire of contrasts.

β. Henry's personal interests more closely connected with France than with England.

γ. This empire was bound to fall to pieces as the feeling of nationality grew in France.

II. Henry and England.

A. He saw the need of maintaining the royal supremacy which he successfully asserted over the clergy and nobles who claimed privileges inconsistent with the constitutional development of the country.

B. He continued the work of organising the government of the country, following the example of his grandfather, Henry I.

C. In spite of occasional harshness (e.g. in the administration of the Forest Laws) he gave England peace, and did much to ensure justice between man and man.

D. Although he attached more importance to his Continental possessions than to England, the able ministers whom he wisely selected did much to promote the best interests of this country.

H

III. **Henry's Personal Character—most Important.**

   A. Fierce temper, strong passions, irreligious, immoral, a typical Angevin—of whom a chronicler said : " From the devil they came ; to the devil they will go "—hence his later estrangement from Eleanor.

   B. An excellent business man. Energetic, methodical, and practical. A great organiser and administrator.

   C. His love of hunting partly explains his policy regarding the forests.

   D. A feudal king (although he weakened the power of the feudal barons in England). He refused to attack the town of Toulouse because Louis VII, his feudal superior, was in it.

   E. Not a man of high ideals. He resolved to be a strong king, but with this exception it is doubtful if he had a clear and definite policy, and whether he fully realised the opportunity afforded by his Continental dominions.

References :

   A. " Henry II." *Twelve English Statesmen*, chap. i.

RICHARD I AND THE THIRD CRUSADE, 1189

I. **The Fall of Jerusalem.**

   A. The Latin kingdom of Jerusalem was weakened by the reign of Baldwin IV (1174–1185), a leper, and of Baldwin V (1185–1186), a child, and by the dispute between the latter's successor, King Guy of Lusignan, and Count Raymond of Tripoli.

   B. Degeneration of the people owing to the luxury of Eastern life. " The Latins of the East had forsaken God, and God now forsook them."

   C. Saladin, a great soldier and diplomatist, by the conquest of Egypt, Aleppo, and Damascus united the divided Moslem States, routed King Guy and captured the True Cross at Hattin and took Jerusalem 1187.

II. **Henry II and Philip Augustus took the Cross in 1188**
owing to the preaching of William Archbishop of Tyre,
the famous historian of the Third Crusade, but mutual
jealousy prevented them from going to Palestine.

    1188. The Saladin Tithe was levied by Henry to meet the
expenses of a crusade.

        α. The first tax levied on personal property (all
previous taxation had been put on land).

        β. Assessed and collected by juries (page 89).

III. **Richard I, a typical Knight-errant, the leading figure in
the Third Crusade.**

    A. To raise money Richard " exposed for sale everything he
had."

        1. Sale of royal offices.

            α. William of Longchamp, Bishop of Ely, pur-
chased the chancellorship for £3000.

            β. Hugh de Puiset, Bishop of Durham, bought
the justiciarship.

            γ. Large sums paid by the sheriffs for their offices.

        2. The freedom of Scotland sold to William the Lion
for 10,000 marks.

        3. Richard took large sums of money from the Jews.

    B. Richard's journey to Palestine.

        (1) **1190.** At Vezelai he made a new alliance with Philip
Augustus and went to Sicily.

        (2) **1191.** In Sicily.

            α. Betrothed to Berengaria of Navarre. Anger of
Philip, to whose sister Adela he had been
previously betrothed.

            β. Supported Tancred in his claim to the throne
of Sicily. Anger of the rival claimant, the
Holy Roman Emperor, Henry VI.

(3) 1191. Conquered Cyprus owing to the cruelty shown
by King Isaac to English sailors and married
Berengaria at Limasol.

(Gave Cyprus to Guy of Lusignan, under whose successors it became a most valuable bulwark against
the Turks.)

(4) 1191. Richard captured Acre, quarrelled with
Leopold of Austria, whose banner he tore down
from the .walls and who went home in consequence.
Philip returned to France. The Saracens were routed
at Arsuf by Richard. Fortification of Ascalon as a
base of operations against Jerusalem.

1192. The French troops deserted Richard and returned to
Acre. Richard advanced within sight of Jerusalem, but
his army was too weak to attack it. Richard relieved
Joppa and made a truce for three years with Saladin,
who allowed the Christians to visit the Holy Sepulchre.

Richard checked Saladin's progress, and by his military successes delayed the inevitable fall of the Latin
kingdom of Jerusalem. (The end came with the
capture of Acre by the Turks in 1291.)

IV. **Richard's return from the Crusades and subsequent History.**
His return due to fear of treachery on the part of John
and of intrigues of Philip Augustus.

A. Richard was shipwrecked in the Adriatic and captured in
Vienna by Leopold of Austria. Leopold gave him up
to the Emperor, Henry VI, who kept him a prisoner
for thirteen months.

B. Successful resistance in England (led by Queen Eleanor)
and in Normandy to the attacks of John and Philip.

C. 1194. Richard released, in spite of the efforts of Philip
and John to induce the Emperor to keep him in
prison, on payment of 150,000 marks and the
acknowledgment of the Emperor's suzerainty over
England.

D. May, 1194. Richard left England (never returned). John
submitted and was kindly received.

E. War with Philip continued more or less until the death of Richard.

   1196. By the Treaty of Gisors, Philip secured the Vexin commanding the entrance to Normandy.

   1196. Richard strengthened Normandy by building Château Gaillard (Saucy Castle) on the Seine.

   1197. Richard formed an alliance, including his nephew Otto, King of the Germans (son of Henry the Lion), and the Counts of Champagne, Boulogne, and Flanders against Philip.

   1198. Richard routed Philip at Gisors. Philip was nearly drowned in the River Epte. "I have made Philip drink deep of the waters of the Epte."

   1199. Richard slain at Chaluz, which he had besieged, owing to the refusal of his vassal the Count to give up treasure he had found which Richard needed to pay the expenses of his war against Philip.

References :

   A. Story of the Nations. *The Crusades*, pp. 304–48.

   C. *The Talisman*, Sir Walter Scott.

THE CONSTITUTIONAL IMPORTANCE OF THE REIGN OF RICHARD I

I. The Reign of Henry II closes the Feudal Period of English History.

   A. England gradually became the most important part of the Angevin dominions.

   B. The system of government founded by Henry was continued in the reign of Richard, whose long absence threw the direction of affairs into the hands of his ministers, under whom that system was extended.

II. The Deposition of Longchamp.

William of Longchamp, Bishop of Ely and Chancellor, was hated
by the barons (especially Hugh de Puiset, the high-born
Bishop of Durham, and Geoffrey Archbishop of York,
the illegitimate son of Henry II) because of his tyranny
and low birth. His exactions made him unpopular with
the people, and opposition to him was supported by John
and London.

1191. Deposition of Longchamp for bad government. This

α. Marks the growth of the idea of ministerial
responsibility,

β. Was accomplished by the union of the barons
supported by the Church and people, and the
means which now proved successful against
Longchamp were to prove successful against
John in 1215.

III. The Justiciarship of Hubert Walter, 1194–1198.

A. The Great Carucage of 1198.

A tax of 5s. on each "carucate," or 100 acres, taxes previously imposed upon the hide (120 acres), and a new
survey was made necessary by the change.

(1) Two knights elected in the Shire Court to assist in the
assessment.

(2) The assessment made on the evidence of sworn jurors,
i.e. the jury system—the system by which chosen men
acted as representatives of their locality—which had
been used in the Saladin Tithe to assess personal was
now used in the assessment of real property. (Later
the same system will be used to elect representatives
in Parliament who in time gain the power of granting
money, as distinct from making an assessment to meet
the King's demand, and finally of determining the
method of expenditure.)

B. Growing importance of the knights of the shire and weakening of the power of the sheriff.

    (1) The importance of the former shown by the part assigned them in the assessment of the Great Carucage and by the duty of nominating the Grand Jury, assigned to four knights elected at the Shire Court.

    (2) The power of the sheriffs weakened

1194. By the election in the Shire Court of four "coroners" to reserve cases for the King's justices. This had been previously done by the sheriffs.

1194. The sheriffs were forbidden to act as justices in their own county.

1194. The sheriffs lost the power of nominating Grand Juries.

C. Opposition of Hugh of Lincoln to the heavy burden of military service.

1197. Hugh Bishop of Lincoln refused Hubert Walter's demand for knights to fight in Normandy with Richard on the ground that his lands were not liable to foreign service. Thus, like Becket in **1164** (p. 82), he afforded an important example of successful constitutional resistance to the King's demand.

    Resignation of the justiciarship by Hubert Walter; appointment of Geoffrey Fitzpeter.

IV. The Development of Towns.

The growing importance of the towns was due to national prosperity, to increasing commerce (especially with the East owing to the Crusades), and growth of wealth, which enabled them to buy privileges from king or barons.

A. London.

    (1) Growth of the merchant guild (between **1066** and **1200**) possessing the right of regulating trade, including all traders, exercising a monopoly of local trade.

    (2) **1191.** John and the barons granted a commune or corporation (involving government by mayor and aldermen representing city wards) in return for the support of the Londoners against Longchamp. London thus became a " collective, popular seignory,"

i.e. its corporation stood in the position of a great tenant-in-chief to the King, exercising the rights and owing the obligations of a feudal baron.

It seems probable that the leading men of the merchant guild formed the corporation, and thus the government of the city was an oligarchy administered by a few wealthy burgesses.

(3) The rising of William FitzOsbert **1196**.

This was due to the unfair incidence of taxation upon the craftsmen whose craft guilds (formed to regulate industry in particular trades) were not as yet strong enough to resist the selfish policy of the merchant guild.   Hubert, owing to the need of money for the war against Philip, supported the merchant guild. The death of FitzOsbert, driven by fire from sanctuary in the Church of St. Mary le Bow, weakened Hubert Walter by arousing the enmity of the commons of London and of the clergy.

B. Other towns made good use of the opportunities afforded by the financial needs of the King.   London alone obtained the full position of a " commune," and London did not keep this position permanently.   But other towns became important owing to the charters they secured, by which they obtained different rights and privileges, such as freedom from toll, exemption from the external jurisdiction of the shire and hundred courts, the election of their own magistrates.

References :

A. Stubbs' *Constitutional History*, Vol. I, pp. 543–51.

B. " Towns."   Medley's *English Constitutional History*, pp. 424–31.

C. For the condition of England :—
    Ivanhoe, Sir Walter Scott.
    In Lincoln Green, by Gilliat, Seeley.

THE LOSS OF NORMANDY

I. **Growing National feeling in France made the loss inevitable.**

II. **Events leading up to the Loss.**

A. Philip Augustus made excellent use of his opportunity to support the rival of the English King. Arthur of Brittany did homage to Philip for Anjou, Maine, and Touraine.

B. **1199.** Philip quarrelled with Innocent III owing to his repudiation of his wife Ingeburga of Denmark for his mistress Agnes of Meran. Owing to this quarrel Philip made a treaty recognising John as heir of *all* Henry II's French fiefs, including Brittany.

C. John should have used his opportunity, but failed.

   (1) He was immoral, false and cruel, therefore hated in England and France.

   (2) He divorced his wife Hadwisa of Gloucester (thus offending the powerful Gloucester family) and married Isabella of Angoulême, betrothed to Hugh the Brown, son of the Count de la Marche, thus

       a. Broke his feudal contract with very powerful vassals,

       β. Gave the Lusignans "a legal right of appeal to their suzerain and a moral right to rebellion."

   1201. *γ.* Agnes of Meran died. Philip made peace with the Pope.

D. John was summoned to Philip's court to answer complaints made against him by the barons of Poitou. He refused to attend, and was deprived of his fiefs, not because of the complaints, but because he refused to obey the summons of his feudal superior.

E. War.

 (1) Arthur was captured at Mirabeau and then disappeared There was no actual knowledge of the facts, but no one suggested that John was incapable of murdering Arthur, and the belief that he was responsible greatly weakened his position.

 (2) Normandy was easily overrun.

 1204. The capture of Château Gaillard and Rouen was soon followed by the loss of the duchy.

  a. The general prevalence of treason made defence impossible.

  β. The growing feeling of nationality in France affected Normandy.

  γ. John, although often an energetic soldier, now became careless; he could trust no one, and seemed to lose all power of action.

 (3) Touraine and Poitou were captured by Philip, but Gascony was saved.

F. 1204. The death of his mother, Eleanor—experienced, diplomatic, and loyal to the Angevins—was a great blow to John.

III. Results of the Loss of Normandy.

A. A great blessing for France and a remarkable triumph for Philip. All the recent conquests except Brittany were incorporated in the Royal domain—consequent increase in the power of the monarchy.

B. A great blessing for England.

 (1) The Norman kings had valued Normandy as much as England, and since 1154 England had been merely a province of the Angevin Empire.

 (2) Now, England stood alone (except for Aquitaine); the feeling of nationality was growing owing to the inter-marriage of Normans and Saxons and to the unity of England under strong kings, and later England, owing partly to this unity, became one of the leading European kingdoms.

C. Great effect on the position of the English nobles.

    (1) They had to choose between allegiance to French and English kings.

    (2) They became English and showed their national sympathies by defending the interests of England in the struggle with John.

D. The loss of Normandy was a great blow to John's personal influence.

References :

    A. *The Political History of England, 1066–1216,* by Adams, pp. 390–406.

    C. *Philip Augustus,* by James, Routledge.

FROM THE LOSS OF NORMANDY TO MAGNA CARTA

I. **The Death of Hubert Walter, Archbishop of Canterbury, 1205,** removed a restraining influence over John, who, on hearing the news, exclaimed, "Now am I King of England!"

II. **John and Innocent III.**

    A. Election of Hubert's successor 1205.

        (1) The monks of the cathedral objected to the interference of the bishops of the province in the election of archbishops, and to the King's claim to appoint archbishops, and elected their sub-prior Reginald.

        (2) The bishops and the King strongly objected to this election, and the monks, annoyed by the foolish conduct of Reginald, then elected the King's nominee, John de Grey, Bishop of Norwich.

        (3) Innocent III ordered a commission of the chapter to come to him to settle the question, and refused to recognise either John de Grey or Reginald. Innocent III nominated his own candidate, Stephen Langton.

           John was very angry. He expelled the monks and confiscated their lands

B. John wanted money. The feudal revenues proved inadequate, and therefore he put a tax on the incomes of beneficed clergy. Innocent put the country under an interdict **1208**. The property of the clergy who obeyed was confiscated by the King.

The struggle between John and Innocent III showed the enormous power of the monarchy. In spite of great unpopularity, tyranny, the badness of his cause, and the interdict, John resisted successfully until forced to yield by a combination of internal disaffection and foreign war in **1213**.

C. The period of successful resistance **1208–1213**.

(1) John's power due to

α. Tyranny. He took hostages from the barons, crushed under sheets of lead the Archdeacon of Norwich who opposed him, and starved to death the wife and son of William de Braose, another opponent.

β. John introduced foreign mercenaries led by Gerard d'Athies and Fawkes de Breauté.

γ. Lack of unity and jealousy between the barons. But the tyranny of John soon caused the barons to unite, and the union of the barons is one of the most important features in the history of the thirteenth century.

(2) Great successes in Wales, Scotland, and Ireland.

1209. α. Scotland. William the Lion submitted, and John got the marriages of his children.

1210. β. Ireland. Captured Carrickfergus and drove out the rebellious Lacies. The native kings swore allegiance at Dublin.

1211. γ. Wales. John defeated Llewellyn.

(3) **1209.** John was excommunicated by Innocent III.

But the King was so strong that the excommunication could not be published at all in England. All the barons attended the Christmas court in **1209**. Homage was renewed by all the free tenants of England and Wales.

(4) **1212.** Alliance with his nephew the Emperor, Otto IV, the Count of Boulogne, Ferdinand of Portugal, and the princes of North-East France, against Philip, as a preliminary to the recapture of Normandy. Most skilful diplomacy on John's part.

D. Submission to Papacy May 13th, **1213.**

(1) Causes.

α. Revolt in Wales and much disaffection in England. Two barons, Fitzwalter and de Vescy, refused a further oath of loyalty and fled.

Peter of Pontefract prophesied John's speedy deposition.

β. Innocent III authorised Philip Augustus to deprive John of the kingdom.

γ. John had no confidence in his army, and Philip's fleet was ready.

(2) Actual submission.

John surrendered the kingdom to the Pope, paid homage to Pandulf; accepted Langton as archbishop; reinstated the exiled clergy and compensated them for their losses.

α. The acknowledgment of the Pope's supremacy was probably a voluntary act of John's.

β. Nothing else would have saved him.

γ. It was not an act of degradation, most kings were vassals, e.g. Richard I **(1194)** became a vassal of the Empire.

δ. No objection was raised to this act during the later rebellion, and possibly John's submission was made with the consent of the barons.

(3) Grave danger to the kingdom arose from the alliance of John and the Pope, and the necessity of limiting the royal power was made clear. Hence Magna Carta, the work of the united nation (Baronage, Church, and People).

Reference :

A. *Short History of the English People*, pp. 122–7.

MAGNA CARTA, 1215

I. The Absolute Power of John.

In the reign of John the monarchy became absolute, owing to the weakening of the baronial power and the development of Henry II's system of centralised government. But under Richard I and John there was also a growing disposition to question the King's right to absolute power, and the barons gradually learned the necessity of uniting the whole nation in resistance to the King.

II. The Battle of Bouvines.

John, having made peace with the Pope, determined to win back Normandy and Poitou from Philip Augustus.

A. 1213. A naval victory gained by William Longsword Earl of Salisbury over the French fleet at Damme saved England from invasion.

B. John determined to attack Poitou while his allies, the Emperor Otto IV and the Counts of Flanders and Boulogne, invaded France from the north.

C. The northern barons refused to serve under an excommunicated King, and, when the excommunication had been removed by Langton, denied their obligation to serve out of England. Their action, theoretically indefensible, was justified by their distrust of the King. John, unable to raise an adequate force, was defeated in Poitou.

D. 1214. Philip routed John's allies at the battle of Bouvines (Flanders), and thus—

α. Ensured his retention of Normandy,

β. Weakened the power of John and facilitated the triumph of his opponents in England. The battle of Bouvines made Magna Carta possible.

III. **The Opponents of the King.**

A. The barons.

(1) The barons were discontented with their loss of power through the growth of absolute monarchy. They had suffered much from John's cruel punishments, heavy exactions, harsh exercise of feudal rights (particularly of wardship and marriage), and, in some cases, from his immoral conduct.

1213. The appointment of Peter des Roches Bishop of Winchester, a servant of John's, to succeed Geoffrey Fitz Peter (who had repeatedly opposed John) as Justiciar, showed the barons that they must depend upon their own efforts.

(2) All the barons united to oppose John, including—

α. The northern nobility (e.g. Peter de Brus and Nicholas de Stutville). These were largely descendants of the lesser nobility of early Norman times, had faithfully supported the kings against the great barons, and bravely resisted the Scots, e.g. at Northallerton, 1138, and Alnwick, 1174. They began the quarrel and supplied the force necessary for success.

β. The descendants of the great Norman barons; Robert FitzWalter, the leader of the baronial army, and the Earls of Hereford and Norfolk.

γ. The connections of the royal family (e.g. William Earl of Salisbury, an illegitimate son of Henry II) and the acting officials of the Curia Regis joined the barons after they reached London.

Pandulf, the Papal Legate, Peter des Roches the new Justiciar, Fawkes de Breauté and Philip, son of Mark, the leaders of John's mercenaries, supported the King to the end.

B. Stephen Langton.

    I. 1213. Produced the Charter of Henry 1 at St. Paul's. This was accepted by the barons as a basis of negotiation.

    II. United clergy, nobles, and people into a party of constitutional reform, and thus made the struggle national, and not merely feudal.

C. The Londoners and the country generally were ready to rebel owing to the exactions of the King and of his foreign mercenaries.

D. Llewellyn ap Iorwerth, Prince of North Wales, anxious to regain the power he had lost owing to John's successful campaign in Wales 1211, joined the barons.

E. Alexander II, King of Scotland, also joined the barons.

IV. Events leading up to the Charter.

    1214. Return of John from Poitou.

        General rising of the barons who met at Bury St. Edmunds, and formally demanded from the King reforms based on the Charter of Henry I.

    1215. John attempted to strengthen his position by hiring mercenaries, fortifying the royal castles, and taking the Cross as a Crusader.

        John tried to win over the Church (and thus to divide his opponents) by promising freedom of election to bishoprics and abbeys.

        Refusal by John of the demands made by the barons, who formally renounced their allegiance and marched from Stamford to London under Robert FitzWalter.

        The barons were joined by the Government officials and the citizens of London.

        Refusal of Langton (who, though a strong supporter of reform, had remained in attendance on the King) to excommunicate John's opponents. John forced to submit.

        Meeting of John and the rebels at Runnymede,

        June 15, 1215. Magna Carta sealed.

V. The Magna Carta.

A. The Church.

> The Church to have freedom of election.
>
> But the King still gave leave to elect bishops and nominated by letters the successful candidate.

B. Limitation of the abuse of feudal rights, of reliefs, wardship, and marriage.

> Reliefs to be fixed.
>
> The guardian of a ward's estate to take only "reasonable expenses."
>
> Heirs to be married "without disparagement" (i.e. without prejudice to their rank or estate).

C. The Commune Concilium to authorise taxation.

> No scutage or aid (except the three regular aids, page 49) to be levied from the King's feudal tenants unless by consent of the Commune Concilium, to which

> (1) Archbishops, bishops, abbots, earls, and greater barons must be summoned individually by writ.

> (2) Other tenants-in-chief to be summoned by a general writ sent to the sheriff.

>> *a.* The clause about taxation protected only the tenants-in-chief, and was omitted from the confirmations of the Magna Carta under Henry III, and this omission was one reason for the discontent of the barons in his reign.

>> **1297.** The Confirmation of the Charters (page 151) provided that certain aids and taxes should not be taken without consent of Parliament (which after 1295 included representatives of cities and boroughs). This was reaffirmed by the Petition of Right, 1628.

>> *β.* The general summons issued to the general body of tenants-in-chief was frequently disregarded, and the greater barons tended to make a selfish use of their power. Hence

I

(1) The justification for the admission to Parliament of representatives of cities and boroughs by Simon de Montfort, 1265, and Edward I, 1295.

(2) When the Houses of Lords and Commons were divided into two Houses in 1341 membership of the former was not conferred by the general summons, and the smaller tenants-in-chief who entered Parliament did so usually as county members of the House of Commons, not as members of the House of Lords. It was these knights of the shire who "fought the battle of the constitution" during the fourteenth century.

D. The Law Courts and justice.

(1) The Court of Common Pleas not to follow the King's Court, but to be held in a fixed place.

A great boon to suitors, who were thus saved from the heavy expense of following the court about the country.

(2) Two justices of the Curia Regis and four knights chosen by the county court to hold assizes four times a year in the shire courts.

(3) The levy of fines.

α. Freemen not to be deprived of the means of earning their living by way of fine, e.g. a merchant's goods not to be taken.

β. Earls and barons to be fined by their peers.

γ. All fines to be in proportion to the offence.

(4) No sheriff, constable, coroner or bailiff of the King to hold the pleas of the Crown, and only men who "know the law" to be appointed as justices, etc.

Thus all serious crimes would be tried before the King's justices—men of good legal knowledge

(5) No royal bailiff to put a man on trial on his bare statement without witnesses.

(6) The "essential clauses" (Hallam).

    a. "No freeman shall be taken or imprisoned or deprived of his property, or outlawed or exiled, or anyways destroyed ; nor will we go upon him, nor will we send upon him, unless by the lawful judgment of his peers or by the law of the land."

    β. "To none will we sell, to none will we deny or delay right or justice."

    These clauses "protect the personal liberty and property of all freemen, by giving security from arbitrary imprisonment and arbitrary spoliation."

    But prisoners were frequently kept in prison a long time before their trial, and to meet this injustice the Habeas Corpus Act was passed in **1679** to ensure speedy trial or release on bail pending trial.

E. Limitation of royal exactions.

(1) Purveyance. (A royal prerogative of purchasing goods for the King's household through the King's purveyors. Great hardship had been caused by the arbitrary exercise of this right.)

    Royal purveyors not to take corn or chattels without payment, or horses, carriages or timber without the owner's consent.

(2) The ferms[1] of counties, hundreds, and tithings not to be increased.

(3) Removal of harsh regulations respecting debts due to the Crown and to the Jews.

F. Forests.

(1) People dwelling outside forests not to be compelled to attend the forest courts.

---

[1] Amount payable yearly to the King.

(2) Afforestments made by John to be deforested.

(3) Twelve sworn knights elected by the county court to make inquiry in each county concerning all "bad customs of the forests."

G. Towns and commerce.

(1) London and all other towns to have all their ancient privileges.

(2) One standard of weights and measures to be fixed for the kingdom.

(3) Merchants to enter, leave, and dwell in England without unfair tolls.

H. Temporary provisions.

(1) Mercenaries to leave the country.

(2) Fair treatment to be given to Llewellyn of Wales and the King of Scotland.

I. The enforcement of Magna Carta.

The whole baronage to elect a council of twenty-five, who, if the King refused to redress the slightest violation of the Charter, should "with the commonalty of the whole land" obtain redress by force, saving harmless the persons of the King, Queen and their children.

This clause implied the duty of the King to keep the laws and asserted the right of his subjects to rebel in case of his refusal to redress violation. It thus denied the right of the King to the absolute power hitherto enjoyed by John.

VI. General Criticism.

A. Magna Carta is of supreme importance in English constitutional history. Hallam called it "the keystone of English liberty"; Chatham asserted that Magna Carta, the Petition of Right, and the Bill of Rights were "the Bible of the English Constitution."

B. The statement that the Magna Carta was "the first public act of the nation after it has realised its own identity" seems inaccurate. A temporary union between the barons, clergy and people was made to resist the tyranny of John, but this did not result in the union of the whole nation. "The idea of the nation, as we now hold it was still in the future, to be called into existence by the circumstances of the next reign." [1]

C. The Magna Carta was the work of the barons, who had been goaded into insurrection by personal wrongs and the way in which John tried to limit baronial rights. The barons fought for themselves, not primarily for the nation.

   (1) But in fighting for themselves the barons did fight for the nation. If John had won there would have been a grave danger that the interests of all classes would have suffered from the establishment of such a monarchical despotism as was actually established in France.

   (2) Although the objects of the barons were purely selfish, they needed the support of the whole nation. The clauses which protected the interests of the church and the people of towns and counties were the price paid for such support, and, with these few exceptions, Magna Carta is feudal in character, and its first object was to protect the interests of the barons.

D. Magna Carta, founded on Henry I's Charter, was conservative. It contained few new elements. But early charters had been vague, and the Magna Carta clearly reasserted old rights.

E. The mention of "communa totius terrae," the commonalty of the whole land, who were to co-operate with the twenty-five barons in maintaining Magna Carta, shows that the people were beginning to be recognised as a factor in politics.

References :

A. *English Constitutional History*, Taswell-Langmead, chap. IV. *Civilisation in the Middle Ages*, Adams. Scribner, pp. 336-340.

   Political History of England, Adams. Longmans, pp. 432 et seq.

B. Stubbs' *Constitutional History*, Vol. II, pp. 2-3.

C. *Runnymede and Lincoln Fair*, by Edgar. Ward, Lock & Co.

[1] Adams, *Political History of England*, p. 437.

KING JOHN'S REVENGE, 1215

I. **John's Acceptance of Magna Carta had been due to Compulsion.**

   He at once attempted to regain his power.

   A. The concession of the Charter broke up the baronial coalition. The northern barons, led by Fitzwalter, had withdrawn from Runnymede and continued their opposition to John, but a number of the nobles, including the Earls of Pembroke and Salisbury, joined him.

   B. Innocent III annulled the Charter. This action was justified by feudal law, because John, as a feudal tenant of the Pope, had no right by concessions to diminish the value of his fief.

   C. The twenty-five barons secured various counties, but John tried to weaken them by appointing his own sheriffs.

   D. John hired more mercenaries, mostly French, fortified the royal castles, and obtained a strong fleet.

   E. Pandulf excommunicated John's leading opponents and suspended Langton, who went to Rome.

II. **John's Early Successes.**

   John captured Rochester, subdued the northern counties, and captured Berwick.

   1216. The Earl of Salisbury conquered the Midlands. John captured Colchester.

III. **Louis (afterwards Louis VIII), son of Philip Augustus, and the English Crown.**

   A. The opponents of John were too weak to resist him, and foreign help was necessary. The choice of Louis due

   (1) To the reluctance of John's French mercenaries to fight against the son of their own King.

   (2) Louis had married Blanche of Castile, granddaughter of Henry II.

   (3) Louis would have been proclaimed King of England in 1213 if Philip's proposed interference had proved successful.

B. Louis asserted
  (1) That John's right to the throne had been rendered void by his condemnation for treachery to Richard and that the crown belonged to Blanche;
  (2) That John had been condemned for the murder of Arthur;
  (3) That he (Louis) was not bound by the treaty Philip Augustus had made with John.

C. Louis landed in Thanet (a storm had destroyed John's fleet), entered London, where the barons paid homage, and captured Winchester. Gallant defence of Dover against Louis by Hubert de Burgh. John was weakened by the desertion of many of the earls (including William of Salisbury, not William the Marshal, Earl of Pembroke), and of his French mercenaries, who would not fight against Louis, and retreated to Shrewsbury. He marched to Lincoln, laying waste the Midlands, raised the siege of Lincoln, gained a victory at Lynn, but lost all his baggage when crossing the Wash. October 19th, 1216. Death of John at Newark, owing to surfeit of peaches and ale and vexation at the loss of his baggage. He named Henry as his heir and the faithful William the Marshal as Henry's guardian.

THE REIGN OF HENRY III
TO THE FALL OF HUBERT DE BURGH,
1216–1232

I. The Administration of William the Marshal, Earl of Pembroke, "Rector regis et regni," 1216–1219.

William the Marshal was supported by Gualo the Papal Legate, the Earls of Chester and Derby, the lords of the Welsh Marches, Hubert de Burgh, the royal officials, and Fawkes de Breauté.

1216. Henry crowned at Gloucester.

A. **1216.** Magna Carta confirmed at Bristol.

    (1) The clauses deciding the constitution of the Great Council and giving the Council control over taxation were omitted because it was thought unwise to hamper the Government in a time of great danger.

    (2) But the acceptance of Magna Carta by the Papal Legate and the Marshal made it permanent. The effect of the original issue had been greatly weakened by its repudiation by Innocent III.

B. The expulsion of the French.

    Growing feeling of national opposition to Louis, now excommunicated by the Pope. Desertion of Louis by many English barons, including William of Salisbury.

    1217. The French routed at Lincoln Fair by the Marshal.

    1217. Hubert de Burgh defeated the French fleet off Dover. He got to windward and threw powdered quicklime in their faces.

    1217. Treaty of Lambeth.

    (1) All Louis' English supporters to be restored to their lands and to pay homage to Henry.

    (2) All towns and castles held by Louis to be given up to the King.

    (3) William the Marshal paid Louis 10,000 marks.

    Departure of Louis and general pacification in England.

C. **1217.** Second issue of the Bristol Charter.

    Issue of a Charter of the Forests deforesting forests recently made and cancelling many of the harsh forest regulations made by Henry II.

    1219. Death of William the Marshal.

D. The importance of his work.

    (1) He established the Magna Carta as a permanent part of the constitution.

(2) He expelled the French.

But this could not have been done without the strong support of Gualo, the loyal barons, and Fawkes de Breauté. Owing to that support—

α. The Papacy gained great influence in England, but hostility was aroused owing to the harsh treatment by Gualo of Louis' clerical supporters.

β. The loyal barons and Fawkes de Breauté became dangerously powerful owing to the large grants with which their support was rewarded.

II. **Hubert de Burgh became Regent on William the Marshal's death in 1219.**

A. **1223.** He compelled William of Aumale and the Earl of Chester to give up royal castles and thus weakened the old baronial party.

B. His main object was to restore the administration to Englishmen, and his policy was " England for the English."

(1) **1224.** Fawkes de Breauté's castle of Bedford was captured and Fawkes driven out of England in spite of the support he had given to William the Marshal.

(2) **1227.** Peter des Roches and his Poitevin friends banished.

(3) Hubert strongly opposed the extension of Papal influence in England.

1221. On the departure of Pandulf (who had succeeded Gualo as Papal Legate) the Pope promised that no Legate should be sent to England during the lifetime of Langton, the supporter of Hubert.

But α. Gregory IX began to give English livings to foreigners, and

1228. β On the death of Langton demanded a tithe of movable property.

1232. Hubert neglected to stop Robert Thweng, who took the money collected from the people by Papal agents and gave it to the poor.

C. Hubert strongly disapproved of Henry III's desire to reconquer the Angevin lands in France. He wished to keep England at peace, and thus to save the heavy expenses of war.

1230. Henry III, in alliance with Pierre Mauclerc of Brittany, who had rebelled against Blanche of Castile (Regent of France for her son, Louis IX), led an unsuccessful expedition to Brittany and Poitou.

1228 and 1231. Failure of expeditions against Llewellyn of Wales.

D. Hubert was the last of the great Justiciars. He tried to restore the system of Henry II, but the development of the constitution was inconsistent with the absolute power of the King, and made the justiciarship of less importance than in the past.

E. The fall of Hubert **1232**, due to the hatred of the barons, whose power he limited, to the strong opposition of the Papal party, of Peter des Roches (who had returned in **1231**), to the feeling caused by the heavy taxes he had been compelled to levy for the King's wars, and to jealousy of the great wealth he had accumulated.

He was accused of mismanagement of the finances, of dissuading the King from recovering Normandy, and of supporting Thweng. Frivolous charges brought against him included those of poisoning William the Marshal and William Earl of Salisbury, and of magic and witchcraft.

III. **The Constitutional importance of the King's Minority.**

A. It showed that the King was not essential for government.

B. The attack on Hubert de Burgh showed the growth of the idea of ministerial responsibility.

C. The conditions of the regency led to the beginning
of an inner ministerial council as distinct from the
Commune Concilium. The beginning of the idea of a
privy council.

References :

A. Green's *Short History of the English People*, pp. 130–1,
and 141–44.

C. *The Robber Baron of Bedford Castle*, by Foster,
Nelson.

THE CAUSES OF THE RISING OF 1258

I. The King's personal character.

Henry III was weak, unable to carry out a strong
policy; he was lacking in stability of purpose, untrust-
worthy, and continually yielded to the Pope and to favourites. He was unable, owing to poverty, to raise an army of
mercenaries. He had little sympathy with English ways,
though proud of his English ancestry, and seldom trusted
men of English blood.

On the fall of Peter des Roches, 1234, he resolved to
be his own minister, ruling through royal clerks, not
barons. His attempt at "personal government" failed,
because of the natural indolence of Henry and the
inefficiency of his servants, and caused much indignation
among the barons.

II. Papal Aggression.

The King, partly through his religious character,
partly through gratitude to the Church for helping him
to get the throne, partly through weakness, allowed the
Pope too much power. Hubert de Burgh, Richard of
Cornwall, and Grossetête Bishop of Lincoln, opposed in
vain the growth of Papal influence in England.

A. England was heavily taxed for the support of Papal schemes against the Emperor Frederick II. Richard of Cornwall said : " England is like a vineyard with a broken hedge. All steal the grapes."

>   **1229.** One-tenth demanded by Gregory IX on all clerical property. Collected by Master Stephen ; opposed by Robert Twenge.

>   **1240.** Gregory IX demanded 20 % of clerical goods.

>   **1244.** Innocent IV continued the quarrel of his predecessor with the Emperor Frederick II, and sent Master Martin to extort more money from England.

B. Grant of English livings to foreigners.

>   **1240.** Gregory IX demanded that three hundred Roman clerks should be presented to English livings to win over their friends to his cause.

C. Cardinal Otto, the Papal Legate **1237–1241**, in spite of his excellent character, roused opposition. Pandulf had acknowledged the supremacy of Canterbury, but Otto refused and claimed jurisdiction over Scotland also. Great riot at Oxford owing to Otto's demands for money.

III. The King's Foreign Policy.

A. France.

>   Joan of Toulouse (daughter of Raymond) married Alfonse, brother of Louis IX. Louis invested Alfonse with Poitou. Rising of Poitevin lords, who feared the loss of their feudal independence, led by Hugh de Lusignan, Henry's stepfather, and supported by Henry III. Henry III was defeated at Taillebourg and Saintes **1242**.

>   **1243.** Henry gave up his claim to Poitou.

B. Henry married his sister Isabella to Frederick II in the hope of using Frederick to counterbalance the French power, but he also

(1) Allowed the Pope to draw money from England to use against Frederick ;

(2) Allowed Otto to excommunicate Frederick in England ;

(3) **1255.** Accepted the crown of Sicily, part of the dominions of Frederick II, for his son Edmund from the Pope, and agreed to discharge the heavy expenses involved.

C. Gascony.

1248. Simon de Montfort, Earl of Leicester, who had married Henry's sister Eleanor (widow of William the Marshall II), was appointed Governor of Gascony. In spite of Henry's failure to give him adequate support he protected Gascony from foreign foes, and put down the turbulent Gascon barons. The harshness of his successful administration caused great discontent. He was unjustly treated by Henry and resigned the governorship in **1252.**

D. Llewellyn ap Griffith rebelled and became Prince of Wales.

IV. **The Alien Favourites.**

A. The English barons strongly objected to the King's foreign favourites because

α. English money, lands, wardships, and marriages were given to foreigners.

β. The King took the advice of foreigners, not of Englishmen, and thus the importance of the Great Council was diminished.

B. The Poitevin followers of Peter des Roches lost power at the fall of their master **1234.**

C. Henry's marriage to Eleanor of Provence, **1236,** led to the coming of her Provençal relatives.

(1) Her uncle, William of Valence, became Bishop of Winchester.

(2) Her uncle, Peter of Savoy, became Earl of Richmond.

(3) Her uncle, Boniface, became Archbishop of Canterbury.

(4) Richard of Cornwall married Henry's sister-in-law, Sanchia of Provence, and joined the Court party.

D. The Lusignans, children of the King's mother and her second husband, Hugh X of Lusignan, Count de la Marche, ruined by French victories in **1242,** came to England. Another Poitevin invasion.

(1) William of Valence, the King's half-brother, became Earl of Pembroke.

(2) Aymer of Valence, the King's half-brother, became Bishop of Winchester.

(3) Alice of Valence, the King's half-sister, married the Earl of Surrey.

V. The Finances were in a hopeless condition.

Much money was wasted by the extravagant King. Great grants were made to foreigners. Heavy expenses of campaigns in Wales, Poitou, and Gascony. Heavy expenses of the expedition to get the Sicilian crown for Edmund ; this very important because " Alexander IV's demand for the discharge of Henry's obligation had contributed not a little towards focussing the general discontent."

VI. Hopeless misgovernment of the Country.

1257.   Distress caused by bad government was aggravated by bad crops, famine, and the hard winter.

VII. The Position of the English Barons.

Their strong opposition was due to Papal aggression, the King's attempt at personal government, the foreigners, and the financial position. The baronial opposition partly selfish (they wanted to get the government in baronial hands. The Marcher barons failed to support Prince Edward, who had received Chester, against Llewellyn, through fear of the growth of Edward's power and the diminution of their own), partly constitutional. They were supported by Grossetête. In **1254** Simon de Montfort, although a foreigner, became leader of the opposition.

1244. The barons demanded the appointment of a justiciar, a chancellor, and a treasurer by the Great Council. This was to end the personal government.

1248 and 1255. They repeated their request.

1257. They rejected Henry's demand for money, thus compelling reform.

Reference :

A. *Simon de Montfort*, by Prothero, chap. VI.   Longmans.

THE PROVISIONS OF OXFORD, 1258

I. The "Mad Parliament."

This name was given by the King's friends to the Great Council which met at Oxford, June, **1258**.

A. The barons presented petitions complaining of

α. The favour shown to foreign favourites.

β. Interference with ecclesiastical elections.

γ. Illegal exactions of feudal services.

δ. The abuse of purveyance.

B. Joint appointment by the Mad Parliament and the King of a committee of twenty-four which drew up the preliminary articles of reform which were called the "Provisions of Oxford." Henry's nominees included three of his half-brothers and probably his wife's uncle, Archbishop Boniface. Of the baron's nominees Simon de Montfort was the only foreigner, and Walter de Cantilupe, Bishop of Worcester, the only ecclesiastic.

II. The Provisions of Oxford.

A. A Council of Fifteen to advise the King.

B. A Council of Twelve to meet the Council of Fifteen thrice yearly.

C. A Council of Twenty-four to make grants to the King.

D. The original twenty-four to organise the King's household and church.

E. Aliens to be expelled. Royal castles to be surrendered.

III. Criticism.

A. A limited monarchy, foreshadowed in Henry's minority, was established. The King's authority was to be exercised in commission by a body of magnates

magnates alone had power. But there was no
the disruptive tendency, which had been the great
from the early Norman barons.

ns were expelled, the Savoyards went voluntarily,
he Poitevins were driven out by force of arms.

IV. ⸺ tlement led to Division among the Barons.

A. One party led by the Earl of Gloucester was satisfied with
the expulsion of the foreigners. They were not anxious
for reform, and had no sympathy with the lesser feudal
tenants and still less with the towns.

B. The other party led by Simon wanted reform and the
recognition of popular rights. The representatives of
the knights approached Edward, and in consequence by
the provisions of Westminster he carried out reforms and
provided for the proper appointment and control of
sheriffs and for the redress of abuses of the Forest Laws.

Reference :

A. Stubbs' *Constitutional History*, Vol. II, pp. 78–85.

SIMON DE MONTFORT

I. His early life.

The fourth son of Simon de Montfort, who had
crushed the Albigensian heresy in Provence. He
obtained the earldom of Leicester through his grand-
mother, and married Henry III's sister Eleanor, the
widow of William Marshal the Younger, in 1238.
Appointed Seneschal of Gascony, where he repressed
turbulent local barons (e.g. Gaston de Béarn) and put
down the Pastoureaux (dangerous robber bands). The
heavy taxes he imposed, and his harsh rule, made him
unpopular, but he served Henry faithfully. Henry
ungratefully deprived him of office 1252.

II. From 1252 to the Barons' War.

A. Simon returned to England and joined the opposition. Although a foreigner he sympathised with the national party in England, and strongly opposed the King's foreign favourites, the aggression of the Pope, the acceptance of the kingdom of Sicily for Edmund, and the King's misgovernment.

B. He took an active part in securing the reforms of the Provisions of Oxford **1258**, but wished the nation and not the barons alone to reap the benefit. He therefore quarrelled with the Earl of Gloucester, the leader of the barons, and was supported by Prince Edward.[1]

C. **1259.** He negotiated the Treaty of Paris, by which Henry gave up his claim to Normandy, Anjou, Touraine, and Maine, but was recognised as Duke of Aquitaine, and agreed to pay homage to Louis IX for Gascony.

D. Although Henry's repudiation of the Provisions of Oxford tended to unite the opposition for a time, the royalist party now led by Prince Edward grew stronger owing

1262. *a.* To the acceptance of the Provisions by Henry.

β. To the imperious temper of Simon and the violence of his sons, which alienated many supporters.

γ. To the adhesion of the Marcher nobles, especially Roger Mortimer, Lord of Wigmore.

1264. δ. To the refusal of Simon to accept the Mise of Amiens, by which Louis IX, to whom, with Simon's consent, the dispute had been referred for arbitration, annulled the Provisions.

---

[1] The title "Prince Edward" is not strictly correct; he was known to his contemporaries as "The Lord Edward."

III. **The Barons' War.**

Simon was supported by a few of the barons (including Hugh le Despenser the Justiciar, and, at first, the young Earl of Gloucester, son of his old opponent), many of the clergy, the Londoners, the Cinque Ports, the friars, the common people, and Llewellyn ap Griffith, Prince of North Wales (with whom he made an alliance to counteract the support given to Prince Edward by the Marcher lords).

1264. Rebellion of London.

Henry captured Northampton and Nottingham and relieved Rochester.

Henry was defeated and captured at Lewes.

α. The victory was gained not by the barons but by Simon's personal adherents.

β. Simon was now dictator.

1264. The Mise of Lewes. A Council of Nine (practically nominated by Simon) to attend and advise the King. Strong opposition of the Pope. The Marcher lords and Queen Eleanor tried now to raise an army in France.

IV. **"Earl Simon's Parliament," 1265.**

Consisted of five earls, eighteen barons, one hundred and twenty clergymen, two knights from every shire, and two burgesses from certain cities and boroughs.

A. "Earl Simon's Parliament" was not a Parliament. The writs were issued by the King, but only to Simon's supporters (e.g. the Archbishop of Canterbury was not summoned).

B. The attendance of the Knights of the Shire in Parliament was not new. They had been summoned before in 1254, and by Simon in 1264.

C. The representatives from the cities and boroughs attended Parliament for the first time. The reeve and four men from each township had been summoned to an assembly at St. Albans in 1213, but it is very doubtful if this assembly met.

(1) Their attendance shows the difference between the policy of Simon and the baronial oligarchy.

(2) Simon treated the representatives of cities and boroughs as a separate estate from the Knights of the Shire, sending the writs for the election of the former to the mayor of each town, and those for the election of the latter to the sheriff.

In Edward I's Great and Model Parliament, **1295**, both burgesses and knights were elected in the county court and formed the third estate.

(3) Thus Simon was not strictly the "Creator of the House of Commons," but his recognition of the political importance of towns made his "Parliament" an important link between the old baronial councils and the later Parliaments.

V. The Battle of Evesham, 1265, and the End of the War.

A. Quarrel between Simon and the young Earl of Gloucester. Escape from captivity of Edward ~~Prince of Wales,~~ who, strongly supported by Gloucester, Roger Mortimer, and the Marcher Lords, became the leader of the baronial party. He promised to maintain the Charters and Provisions of Oxford against Simon, whose power seemed dangerous to King and barons.

B. **1265.** Edward defeated Simon's son at Kenilworth.

Edward defeated and slew Simon and Hugh le Despenser the Justiciar at Evesham, and slaughtered many Londoners.

1266. The Cinque Ports submitted.

C. **1266.** Fresh risings owing to the confiscation of the property of Simon's adherents, therefore called "The Disinherited."

The younger Simon formed a camp of refuge in the Isle of Axholme, stirred up the Cinque Ports, but finally submitted at Kenilworth.

D. Milder terms were now offered to the rebels owing to the conciliatory policy of Edward and Gloucester, and in spite of the opposition of Roger Mortimer, the leader of the extreme section of the barons who quarrelled with Gloucester.

1266. The Ban of Kenilworth.

(1) The Disinherited to redeem their estates by paying a fine equivalent to five years' income.

(2) The Charters re-enacted.

(3) The King's authority reasserted.

(4) Simon not to be reputed a saint.

The Earl of Gloucester, fearing the designs of Roger Mortimer, took up arms to maintain the Ban of Kenilworth.

1267. Submission of the last of the Disinherited in the Isle of Ely, and general pacification.

E. **1267.** Statute of Marlborough.

Re-enacted the Charters and Provisions of Oxford.

F. **1267.** Treaty of Shrewsbury, between Llewellyn and Henry.

Llewellyn was recognised as Prince of Wales, on condition of paying homage to Henry, and received large grants in Denbigh and Flint.

These favourable terms were due to Edward's desire for peace, but Llewellyn became so strong that the Welsh Wars of Edward I (**1277** and **1282**) were made inevitable.

1267–1272. Peace for the rest of Henry's reign.

1270. Prince Edward went on the Crusade.

VI. Simon de Montfort.

A. Although a foreigner he became the champion of the English people and rendered great service to England.

(1) He helped the cause of constitutional development by supporting the commons against the barons.

(2) Resisted the unconstitutional power of foreign favourites.

(3) Opposed the interference of the Pope.

B. The work of Simon was carried on by Edward I, who confirmed the principles asserted by Simon.

C. His private character.

   (1) Determined, steady of purpose, and true to his principles. He " stood like a pillar."

   (2) Patriotic and devoted to the interests of England.

   (3) Pious, a great friend of Grossetête, and a supporter of the friars. " Earl Simon the Righteous."

   (4) Masterful ; hot-tempered. " Not a saint, but a man of a great heart."

References :

A. *Simon de Montfort*, by Prothero, Longmans, chap. x.

B. *Short History of the English People*, pp. 152–4.

C. *A Clerk of Oxford*, by Everett Green, Nelson, and *Forest Days*, by James, Routledge.

EDWARD I AND WALES

I. **Llewellyn ap Griffith, 1254–1282** (grandson of Llewellyn ap Jorwerth), Lord of Gwynedd, aimed at conquering the whole of Wales and making it independent of England. His plans checked by the grant to Edward by Henry III of Cheshire, the four Cantreds (Flintshire and Denbighshire), Cardigan and Caermarthen.

A. His early success.

   He took advantage of a national rising caused by an attempt to set up shire courts and to suppress Welsh judicial institutions in the Cantreds, Cardigan and Caermarthen. Conquered the Cantreds and Cardigan and gained much land on the upper Wye and Severn. Took the title of " Prince of Wales." His success due partly to the apathy of the Marcher Lords, who strongly resented the grants made by Henry III to Edward.

B. Supported Simon de Montfort, and by the Treaty of Shrewsbury, **1267**, was accepted as Prince of Wales on condition of paying homage to Henry III, was granted the Four Cantreds and much land in Middle and South Wales.

His success roused the fear of the Marcher Lords and the jealousy of some of the smaller Welsh chiefs, but he maintained his power.

II. The First Welsh War.

1272. The death of Henry III and absence of Edward from England encouraged Llewellyn to renounce his homage to the King of England, which was inconsistent with the independence of Wales.

1275. Edward captured Eleanor, daughter of Simon de Montfort, on her way to marry Llewellyn, and kept her at his court.

1277. Edward invaded Wales. Prompt submission of Middle and South Wales. Capture of the Four Cantreds. Retreat of Llewellyn to Gwynedd. Capture of Anglesea by Edward, with the help of a fleet from the Cinque Ports, and submission of Llewellyn. The Treaty of Conway.

(1) Llewellyn gave up all his conquests, including the Four Cantreds,

(2) And agreed to do homage and pay a heavy indemnity. Llewellyn thus became "a petty North Wales chieftain" instead of Prince of Wales, and was allowed to marry Eleanor de Montfort.

III. The Second Welsh War.

A. Edward failed to appreciate the attachment of the Welsh to their old laws and customs, and tried to introduce English laws and English shire courts. The harshness of his agents aggravated the resentment of the Welsh, and Edward's oppression roused national opposition and led to the union of Wales.

B. **1282.** Second rising of Llewellyn and his brother David, who had previously supported Edward.

> Capture by David of Hawarden and Aberystwith castles.

> Llewellyn was gradually driven into Gwynedd,

1282. But escaped and was slain at Builth while trying to organise a rising in South Wales, and the struggle was now confined to Gwynedd, where David held out.

1283. Edward, after great difficulties and with the help of Gascon soldiers, captured David, who was executed for treachery at Shrewsbury.

> The story of the massacre of the Welsh bards by Edward is not true.

IV. The Second Settlement.

A. The Legal Settlement.

(1) The Statute of Wales, **1284**, issued at Rhuddlan ensured the organisation of the Welsh Counties.

> α. The Snowdon district was divided into Anglesea, Carnarvon, and Merioneth.

> β. Reorganisation of the counties of Cardigan and Carmarthen.

> γ. The county of Flint attached to the Earldom of Chester.

(2) English law, particularly criminal law and the law of inheritance, was administered in the shire courts, but sympathy was shown to Welsh national feeling and many old customs were allowed to continue. This partly accounts for the permanent nature of the second settlement.

1284. Edward's infant son, born at Carnarvon, proclaimed "Prince of Wales."

B. Castles.

New "concentric" (as distinguished from Norman) castles built at Conway, Carnarvon, and Harlech to dominate Gwynedd, and at Caerphilly and Kidwelly to hold South Wales. These became the nucleus of English towns.

C. The subjugation of Wales removed the necessity for the continuance of the great power of the Marcher Lords. They held their authority until the reign of Henry VIII, but the success of Edward rendered it impossible for them to extend their power, and in course of time many of the marcher principalities passed to the Crown.

D. Wales was not directly annexed to England by Edward I. It remained under the immediate authority of the Crown until **1536**, when it was united to England and sent members to Parliament for the first time.

E. The Ecclesiastical Settlement.

Archbishop Peckham built churches, protected ecclesiastical property, made provision for training clergy, and put down simony and the marriage of the clergy.

References :

A. " Edward I." *Twelve English Statesmen*, chap. VI.

B. *The Bard*, Gray.

C. *The King's Reeve*, by Gilliat, Seeley.

EDWARD I AND SCOTLAND

I. The Maid of Norway.

A. **1286.** Death of Alexander III, King of Scotland, who had married Edward's sister Margaret.

B. Alexander's daughter Margaret had married Eric, King of Norway, and her daughter Margaret, "The Maid of Norway," was proclaimed Queen of Scotland.

C. The Treaty of Brigham, 1290, between Edward I and the Scotch, provided for the marriage of Prince Edward and Margaret, and the maintenance of Scottish customs. Scotland to remain "separate and divided from England."

A wise scheme, aiming at unity through personal union of the two crowns.

D. 1290. Death of the Maid on her voyage from Norway to Scotland.

II. **The Decision in favour of Balliol.**

A. Thirteen claimants to the crown appeared. Question whether Scotland
   (1) Should be divided, or
   (2) Should be given to one claimant, and to which.

B. No one in Scotland was strong enough to decide. Therefore an appeal was made to Edward I, who asserted his claim to the overlordship of Scotland.
   (1) The kings of England since Henry II had asserted this claim in spite of Richard I's sale of the homage of Scotland to William the Lion in 1189.
   (2) The homage paid by Scottish kings had been (except in the case of William the Lion) done for lands held in England by the kings of Scotland, especially for the earldom of Huntingdon.
   (3) Edward levied an army and the claimants did homage to him at Norham 1291. The royal castles were surrendered, i.e. Edward's success was due to force.
   (4) The Scots did not think that his suzerainty would be a reality, but Edward thought that the agreement of Norham meant that England had annexed Scotland and that his authority was thus established over the whole of Great Britain.

C. The final decision of the judges in favour of Balliol showed
   (1) That they favoured primogeniture as against proximity of blood.
   (2) That they regarded the kingdom of Scotland as indivisible.

D. Edward had established his supremacy over Scotland, but had given the Scots a preponderating voice in the tribunal which considered the claim to the throne; he resisted the temptation to split up the kingdom, and now restored the castles. He had not as yet provoked much resistance in Scotland or roused national feeling.

III. The Struggle with Balliol 1295.

A. Appeals from Scotch to English courts, unknown before, caused great dissatisfaction.

B. 1295. Balliol made an alliance with France which was 1294–1297 engaged in a struggle with Edward about Gascony (pages 139–142).

C. The Scots refused to surrender the border castles to Edward I.

D. Balliol renounced his vassalage.

(Edward to strengthen his hands summoned the Great and Model Parliament in 1295.)

E. War.

Edward's command of the sea greatly facilitated the transport of men and material of war. His victory at Dunbar 1296 was followed by the conquest of southern Scotland. Earl Warrenne made governor, Cressingham treasurer, and William Ormesby justiciar.

Balliol by his alliance with France and by renouncing his vassalage had given Edward ample justification for his action according to feudal law.

IV. The Struggle with Wallace.

A. The rapacity and cruelty of English officials led to the rising of Wallace, who defeated the English at Stirling 1297.

1298. Edward routed Wallace at Falkirk.

There was no permanent conquest even in the Lowlands, and the English castles were soon besieged. The Scottish barons, who had been unwilling to fight under Wallace, a lowborn leader, now combined. John Comyn was made regent and the Scottish nobles took up the national cause.

B. The second conquest of Scotland **1304.**

      Stirling captured and Wallace executed, **1305.** Edward's nephew, the Earl of Richmond, made governor. Justices and sheriffs appointed, Celtic laws abolished. The Scottish Parliament kept. The claim of Boniface VIII to suzerainty over Scotland denied.

      An excellent scheme, but their love of independence prevented the Scots from accepting the supremacy of a foreign king.

V. **Further rising under Bruce. Death of Edward I at Burgh on Sands 1307.**

Edward's Scottish policy failed owing to national resistance.

References :

    A. " Edward I." *Twelve English Statesmen*, chaps. x and xii.

    C. *The Scottish Chiefs*, by Porter, Dent.

EDWARD I AND FRANCE

I. **Early Difficulties.**

A. Refusal of Philip III to surrender to Edward I, Limoges, Cahors, and Perigueux (ceded by St. Louis to Henry III), and parts of Saintonge and Quercy rightly claimed by the English.

B. **1273.** Edward paid homage to Philip III " for all the lands which I ought to hold of you."

C. Establishment of Edward's supremacy in Gascony, and submission of Gaston of Bearn, the leader of the discontented Gascon nobles.

D. Edward claimed Ponthieu for his wife, Eleanor of Castile, as heiress of her mother, Queen Joan of Castile.

E. **1279.** Treaty of Amiens.

    (1) Edward gave up his claims to Limoges, Cahors, and Perigueux.

    (2) Philip III recognised Eleanor's right to Ponthieu, surrendered the Agenais, and promised fair consideration for Edward's claim to Quercy.

F. 1287–1289.   Edward reorganised the administration of
Aquitaine, and built "bastides" (fortified towns) to
strengthen his authority.   Consequent development of
commerce (especially in Bordeaux) and closer connection with England.

II. The French War.

A. Bitter rivalry between the sailors of the Cinque Ports and
Norman traders.

1293.   A Norman fleet routed off St. Mahé, in Brittany, by
an English and Gascon fleet.

Edward summoned to Paris by Philip IV (the
Fair) to answer for the action of the English sailors
and for disturbances in Gascony.

Edward was represented by his brother Edmund,
who agreed that part of Gascony should be formally
ceded to Philip for forty days as an acknowledgment
of his overlordship, although he was not to take
actual possession.

B. Owing to Edward's non-appearance he was declared "con-
tumacious," and Philip, in spite of his previous undertaking, took possession of Gascony.

C. Edward's preparations for war.

(1) Attempt to form a coalition against France, including
Brabant, Savoy, and Aragon.

(2) Demand of assistance from the feudal tenants of
England, from Gascony, from Wales, and from the
chief barons of Scotland and Ireland.   But the
Scotch, prompted by the French, refused to serve,
1294.   and the demand for service in Gascony led to
a rebellion in Wales (under Madoc, a bastard son
of Llewellyn ap Griffith).   The necessity of subduing
Wales delayed Edward's operations against France
and overwhelmed him with debt.[1]

---

[1] During his successful campaign in North Wales Edward adopted the
plan of sending forward with his heavy cavalry archers whose arrows broke
up the enemy's lines and made the charge of the cavalry more effective.
These tactics proved most successful in his wars with Scotland and in the
early part of the Hundred Years' War.

(3) Money was raised by the seizure of wool and of the coined money in cathedral treasuries, by contributions from shires and boroughs, and from the clergy, who were compelled to grant half their income. Protest of the Dean of St. Paul's, who fell dead through fear at Edward's feet.

D. The war.

1294-1295. The command of the sea most important. Edward appointed three admirals to command the fleets of the eastern, southern, and western (including Ireland) coasts. The navy was reorganised, and prevented invasion of England.

1295. An expedition to Gascony under Edward's nephew, John of Brittany, captured Bayonne, but failed to reconquer the duchy.

The French burned Dover and the English Cherbourg.

1295. Alliance made between Scotland and France, and betrothal of Edward Balliol to Philip IV's niece Joan. The beginning of the friendship between France and Scotland, which continued for nearly three hundred years.

Consequent delay of Edward's personal intervention in France. The alliance between France and

1295. Scotland led Edward to summon the Great and Model Parliament, in which the lower clergy, counties, cities, and boroughs were represented (p. 149). An attempt to secure the support of the whole nation.

1296. Conquest of Scotland (p. 138), but the King now delayed operations in France owing to the refusal of the clergy to give supplies, and, after their sub

1297. mission, to the refusal of the Earls Marshal (Norfolk) and Constable (Hereford) to serve in Gascony while Edward himself fought in Flanders. The expedition to Gascony was therefore given up, Edward's expedition

1298. to Flanders proved indecisive, but peace was made between England and France by the arbitration of the Pope (in his private capacity), and Edward (whose first wife, Eleanor of Castile, had died in 1290) married Philip's sister Margaret. His son Edward was betrothed to Philip's daughter Isabella.

1303. Philip, engaged in a fierce quarrel with Pope Boniface VIII and at war with the Flemings (who routed his troops at Courtrai 1302), made with Edward the Treaty of Paris, by which Edward received Gascony on condition of paying homage.

THE LEGISLATION OF EDWARD I
TO 1290

I. General Notes.

Edward I, like St. Louis of France, was a great legislator. He continued the work of Henry II by strengthening the royal authority over barons and clergy, and by extending Henry II's judicial organisation.

His work was selective rather than creative. His legislation contains little that is quite new, but he rendered great service to England by defining the rights and duties of different classes. The reign of Edward I was a " period of definition."

II. The Consolidation of the Royal Power.

A. Over the barons.

(1) The regulation of the baronial franchises (i.e. rights of jurisdiction).

1278. The Statute of Gloucester provided that itinerant justices should inquire, in accordance with a writ of Quo Warranto, by what warrant the franchises were held.

a. This involved the idea that all rights of jurisdiction
came from the King, and that he could cancel rights
which were not based on a royal grant.

β. Strong resistance of Earl Warrenne. "By the sword my
ancestors gained their lands, and by the sword I will
defend them."

γ. Very few franchises were abolished, but future extension was prevented, and in consequence baronial
jurisdiction gradually decayed.

(2) The estates of the barons.

a. 1285. The Second Statute of Westminster included the
clause, "De Donis Conditionalibus," which ensured
the succession of heirs to family estates granted con-
ditionally to other holders. The creation of entail.[1]

This statute tended to make permanent the old
system of landholding, and was reactionary in character. But while the barons gladly accepted a law
which ensured the entail of their estates, the King,
being the greatest landholder, derived the greatest
benefit.

β. 1290. The Statute Quia Emptores.

"In all future transfers of land, the purchaser,
instead of becoming the feudal dependent of the
alienor, should enter into the same relations in which
the alienor had stood to the next lord."

1. The object was to prevent loss of services and
feudal profits to the overlord, and especially to
the King, by subinfeudation.

2. By preventing subinfeudation it weakened feudalism, and it strengthened the King by increasing the number of tenants-in-chief holding directly of the Crown.

3. It facilitated the transfer of land, and gave
opportunities of acquiring landed property to
the great merchants.

---

[1] An entailed estate (taillé, limited) was so called because it limited the
holder's right of disposition.

1278. Owing to this statute and to the "distraint of knighthood" (by which all owners of estates worth £20 per annum were to be knighted), there arose a class of country gentry, a non-baronial landowning class, who tended to support the royal power against the barons.

B. Over the clergy.

(1) The Statute of Mortmain, 1279.

α. 1279. Archbishop Peckham had induced a council at Reading to pass canons asserting the rights of the Church as guaranteed in Magna Carta, especially the authority of the ecclesiastical courts, and had ordered Magna Carta to be posted every year on church doors in his province.

The Statute of Mortmain was the King's answer to these canons.

β. The Statute of Mortmain, "statutum de viris religiosis," forbade the grant of land to any corporation, lay or ecclesiastical, in such a way that it "should come into the dead hand."

1. The Church, being a corporation, never died, and lands alienated to the Church thus escaped payment of certain feudal dues, particularly reliefs (page 49), and considerable loss was thus inflicted on the overlord, especially on the King.

2. Landowners had frequently avoided the payment of reliefs by the fraudulent conveyance of land to the Church.

3. The consequent increase in the property of the Church made it too powerful, and it was essential, in the interests of the royal authority, that this power should be curtailed.

(2) The attempt of Peckham to extend the power of the Church Courts.

1281. α. Peckham tried to take all suits respecting patron-
age and the personal property of the clergy out of the
jurisdiction of the royal courts, but was prevented by
the King.

1285. β. Unsuccessful attempt of the clergy to check the
issue of prohibitions from the King's Court on the
prosecution of suits against laymen in Church courts.

(3) The Writ Circumspecte Agatis ("mind what you are
doing"), **1285**, defined the powers of the ecclesiastical
courts, and confined their jurisdiction to matters
merely spiritual (such as questions of marriage, wills,
tithes, churches, and offences for which penance could
be enforced.)

This limited the extension of clerical jurisdiction,
which was part of Peckham's policy.

C. The royal power was defined.

(1) Statute of Westminster (the First), **1275**.

α. Re-enacted and reviewed Magna Carta, the
Provisions of Oxford, and the Statute of
Marlborough.

β. Provided that elections should be free and
that feudal aids should be reasonable in
amount.

(2) Settlement of the customs on wool, woolfells, and
leather, "Magna aut antiqua custuma." The King to
receive half a mark on every sack of wool, half a mark
for every three hundred woolfells,[1] and one mark for
every last of leather exported.

α. Wool was the staple produce of the country and
was easily taxed, e.g. Richard's ransom in **1194**
had been raised largely by the seizure of the
wool of the Cistercian monks.

---

[1] Skins with wool attached.

β. This settlement led to the limitation of the royal power of exacting taxation from English merchants, although

1. It did not prevent the King from obtaining an additional grant if the merchants were willing to make it.

2. The King's power of extorting money from foreign merchants was not limited by the settlement of the "Magna aut antiqua custuma," and in 1303 he gave them certain privileges by the Carta Mercatoria in return for increased grants on wool called the "Parva et nova custuma."

(3) Statute of Westminster (the Second), 1285.

Re-enactment of the Statutes of Gloucester (1278), Mortmain (1279), and others, limitation of abuses of manorial courts, settlement of the land law by the clause "De donis conditionalibus" (page 143).

III. **The maintenance of Peace and the protection of Commerce.**

A. Statute of Winchester, 1285.

(1) Prompt pursuit to be made of criminals from town to town and from county to county.

(2) The inhabitants of hundreds and franchises to be answerable for robberies committed within their borders.

(3) In towns gates to be closed from sunset to sunrise, watches to be kept during the night, bailiffs to make inquiries respecting strangers.

(4) In the country highways to be widened by the clearance of brushwood for two hundred feet each side. (This regulation was made to protect travellers from the arrows of ambushed robbers.)

(5) Every man to be armed according to his rank (the revival of the Assize of Arms, 1181); two constables to hold a view of armour twice a year in every hundred and to present defaulters to justices assigned for the purpose. (These justices, "conservatores pacis," afterwards received judicial powers and were the forerunners of our "Justices of the Peace.")

The Statute of Winchester shows the permanence of the ancient popular law, and revives such old national institutions as the hue and cry, watch and ward, and the Assize of Arms. An excellent example of Edward's skill in adapting old institutions to contemporary requirements.

B. The Statute of Merchants (or Statute of Acton Burnell), 1283, enabled merchants to recover debts. Debtors to be imprisoned or to forfeit their property.

IV. The Organisation of the Judiciary.

A. The Assizes.

(1) Great abuses had arisen during the reign of Henry III.

(2) 1285. The Statute of Westminster (the Second) provided that two judges should try cases at Westminster thrice a year *unless* they had *before* been taken on circuit in the county courts. The origin of "Nisi Prius" cases.

(3) 1293. England divided into four circuits, each with two judges,

a. To take all assizes (criminal and civil), and

β. To sit throughout the year.

This arrangement was a great convenience to suitors owing to the increase in the number of judges, the decrease in expense, the settlement of all kinds of cases, and the permanence of the commission.

B. The development of the Central Courts of Justice.

(1) The growth of the judicial work of the Curia Regis had led to its division into three courts—the Exchequer (dealing with fiscal questions), Common Pleas (fixed at Westminster by Magna Carta, and dealing with civil cases between subject and subject), and the Court of King's Bench (founded in **1178,** and dealing with pleas of the crown).

(2) In the time of Edward I these courts were further organised :

α. Each received its own staff of judges.

β. The abolition of the justiciarship removed a bond of union between the courts.

γ. Their functions were more clearly defined, e.g. the Court of Exchequer was forbidden to try common pleas.

(3) Growth of equitable jurisdiction.

α. The King's Continual or Permanent Council (which had come into importance during the minority of Henry III, and later became the Privy Council) examined and remitted to the proper courts petitions against unjust judgments of the common law courts.

β. Development of the equitable jurisdiction of the Chancellor to deal with cases over which the common law courts had no jurisdiction.

(4) Results.

α. Gradual decay in importance of the local courts and the weakening of the authority of the sheriffs.

β. The organisation of the central jurisdiction gave definiteness to the common law.

References :

A. Stubbs' *Constitutional History*, Vol. II, pp. 109 *et seq.*
Medley's *English Constitutional History*, pp. 367–83.
" Edward I." *Twelve English Statesmen*, chap. VII.

THE GREAT AND MODEL PARLIAMENT, 1295

I. **The immediate cause was Political.**

Edward felt the need of the support of the whole nation to resist the enemies of England—the Welsh (who had rebelled under Madoc in **1294**), the French (who burnt Dover in **1295**), and the Scots, who had just made an alliance with France.

II. **The object was Financial**—to obtain a grant of money to meet the cost of national defence, and grants of one-eleventh, one-tenth, and one-seventh were made by the barons and knights of the shire, the clergy, and the boroughs respectively. No judicial or legislative business was done by this Parliament.

III. **The Constitution.**

The Parliament was composed of representatives of all classes of the community "ut quod omnes similiter tangit ab omnibus approbetur."

A. Members summoned by special writ.

The archbishops, bishops, abbots, earls, and barons received special writs, and the receipt of a special writ of summons became the qualification of a member of the House of Lords, while membership of its predecessor the Commune Concilium had depended on baronial tenure. The receipt of a special writ became a hereditary right, and thus Edward's action led to the settlement of membership of the House of Lords. Edward was thus, to some extent, the "Founder of the House of Lords."

B. Members summoned indirectly.

(1) The lower clergy.

By the "præmunientes" clause the Archbishops of Canterbury and York were "premonished" to ensure the attendance of heads of chapters, archdeacons, two representatives for the clergy of each diocese, and one for the clergy of each cathedral.

α. But the clergy preferred to grant aids in Convocation, and during the fourteenth century ceased to attend Parliament, partly through dislike of obeying a secular summons.

β. The clergy thus did not become a separate estate of the realm.

(2) The representatives of the shires, cities, and boroughs. Two knights from every shire, two citizens from each city, two burghers from each borough to be elected in the full county court in accordance with a general writ issued to the sheriff.

α. The union of the knights of the shire with the burgesses was the foundation of the strength of the House of Commons.

β. The principle of election, used previously for the declaration of local custom (e.g. Domesday Book) for the assessment of taxation (e.g. Saladin Tithe, 1188), was now finally adopted for Parliamentary representation.

Edward united the new system of estates with the old principles of representation.

γ. Edward I was not the "creator of the House of Commons," and his policy of summoning representatives of the cities and boroughs had been anticipated by Simon de Montfort. But "his policy did much to settle the character of that House as being the House of assembled shire moots."

IV. General Notes.

A. The Great and Model Parliament was an excellent example of Edward's "policy of definition." It ensured the adequate representation of the clergy, barons, and people, and afforded a model to its successors.

B. The three estates of clergy, lords, and commons never seemed likely to combine. The clergy soon ceased to attend, and about **1341** the Parliament was sharply divided into two Houses—Lords and Commons.

Reference :

A. Taswell - Langmead, *English Constitutional History*, pp. 206–10.

THE CONFIRMATION
OF THE CHARTERS, 1297

I. The Opposition to the King.

Edward I was attempting to hold Gascony, to make a diversion in Flanders with the help of his ally Guy Count of Flanders against Philip IV, and to conquer Scotland. This task, which was beyond the power of England, led to attempts by the King to raise money and to collect forces to fight in Flanders under Edward himself, and in Gascony under Edmund of Lancaster.

A. Archbishop Winchelsey and the clergy.

(1) **1296.** Boniface VIII, by the bull Clericis Laicos, forbade the clergy to pay taxes to any lay power. This was due—

   a. To the attempt to maintain the independence of the Church.

   β. To the desire to stop wars, the cost of which was largely met by taxes on the clergy.

(2) **1297.** Consequent refusal of Winchelsey to agree to a grant of one-fifth, demanded by Edward.

(3) The clergy outlawed by the King.

(4) Winchelsey excommunicated his opponents.

(5) The King seized Church property.

B. The barons.

(1) The barons were discontented owing to the growing power of the King and his disregard for Magna Carta and the Charter of the Forests.

(2) The death of the old baronial leaders, such as Gilbert of Gloucester, left at the head of their party the Constable, Bohun Earl of Hereford, and the Marshal, Bigod Earl of Norfolk. Both had personal grievances against Edward I, who had punished Hereford for waging private war against Gilbert of Gloucester, and had suspended the Earl Marshal.

(3) The refusal of the clergy to make a grant made an appeal to the barons necessary, but at an assembly of the barons held at Salisbury (Feb., 1297), the Constable and Marshal refused to serve abroad save in attendance on the King; and Norfolk, in reply to Edward's assertion that he should either go to Gascony or hang, declared that he would "neither go nor hang."

  α. The attitude of the barons was narrow and unstatesmanlike. Their objection was based on the comparatively small point of their own feudal obligation to military service.

  β. They failed to appreciate the broader questions of the time and made no mention of illegal taxation or of the proposed illegal use of the national levy for foreign service.

C. The Merchants.

Having failed to secure aid from the clergy and barons, Edward, without any pretence of Parliamentary grant, took money and supplies from the merchants.

(1) He seized wool and hides.

(2) Levied a heavier tax of 40s. per sack on wool. The maletot [male tollita, i.e. unjust tax].

(3) Took stores of corn and meat from the counties.

D. All his opponents united against the King through fear of the loss of rights guaranteed by Magna Carta. The national union which Edward had recognised in the Great and Model Parliament of 1295 was now directed against him, and a movement which hitherto had aimed at the assertion of clerical and feudal immunities became a national rising in defence of English freedom.

II. The Submission of the Clergy.

Edward was bound by his promises to his allies to carry on the war and made terms with the clergy, thus dividing his enemies.

A. Winchelsey allowed the clergy to "follow their own consciences" and to make voluntary contributions to the King. Grant of one-fifth to Edward by the great majority of the clergy.

B. Reconciliation of Edward and Winchelsey, and restoration of the Archbishop's confiscated property.

C. Boniface VIII repealed the bull Clericis Laicos.

III. Continued Opposition of the Constable and Marshal.

A. Some of the barons made a grant of one-eighth to the King, who ordered a military levy of the whole of the kingdom for service abroad.

B. The Constable and Marshal rightly maintained that the national levy was bound to serve only at home, refused to draw up lists of men liable for service, and were superseded by the King.

C. Presentation of a petition to the King by the constable and marshal protesting against the unconstitutional demand for foreign service, the violation of the Charters and the maletot, and demanding that the King should remain at home.

D. August 24th, 1297. Departure of Edward for Flanders, his son, Prince Edward, left as regent.

E. The Constable and Marshal forbade the Exchequer officers
to collect supplies until the Magna Carta and the
Charter of the Forests were confirmed, and denied the
legality of recent grants, i.e. they demanded that
grievances should be redressed before supplies were
granted.

IV. The Confirmation of the Charters.

A. The Prince Regent, on the demand of the earls, confirmed
Magna Carta and the Charter of the Forests, and
accepted additional articles proposed in the form of a
petition. His action was confirmed by King Edward at
Ghent.

B. The additional articles exist in two forms.

(1) The French version is the authentic form, and provided :—

a. No such aids or prises (as those recently taken
and including the maletot on wool) should be
taken but by the common consent of the realm.

β. The King's rights to the "ancient customs" on
wool are expressly reserved.

γ. There is no mention of tallage.

(2) The Latin version is termed "De Tallagio non Conce-
dendo." This was wrongly regarded by the framers
of the Petition of Right, 1628, as a statute, but was
in reality either the original petition presented by the
earls to the regent, or an "abstract of the regent's act
of confirmation." The Latin version is much more
stringent than the French.

a. "No tallage or aid" to be taken without the
consent of the realm.

β. No corn, wool, or leather to be taken without
the consent of the owners.

γ. No reservation is made of the King's rights,

V. General Notes on the Confirmation.

A. A great constitutional victory for the barons. The Confirmation embodies the constitutional progress made since Magna Carta, and shows that the leaders of the people expected to play some part in directing national policy.

B. The Confirmation was due to forces which had been steadily growing, and the union of the nation which ensured it, had been foreshadowed in the Great and Model Parliament, **1295**. But the success of the barons was to some extent the result of the coincidence of the complaints of the clergy, barons, and merchants (none of which had a direct bearing on the Charter).

C. No guaranteeing clauses were inserted in the Confirmation as in the Magna Carta. These were no longer necessary, as the nation recognised the importance of its victory, and was resolved to maintain the advantages it had secured.

Reference :

A. Stubbs' *Constitutional History*, Vol. II, pp. 136–58.

THE EXPULSION OF THE JEWS

I. Their position in the Country.

A. A few Jews lived in England before the Norman Conquest, but there was a considerable immigration in the reign of William the Conqueror, who protected them. They settled in special quarters of towns called Jewries. They were the first traders to build stone houses in England, and this was due to their wealth and to the need of defence against their enemies. "The Jew's House," a Norman dwelling-house, is still standing at Lincoln.

B. The Jews and the King.

    (1) The Jews were "the King's chattels," and he was the absolute owner of their property and persons.

    (2) They paid the King heavy taxes for permission to trade and were used by him "as sponges," being frequently compelled to hand over to the King money obtained from his subjects by trade or usury. They thus became a kind of instrument of indirect taxation and therefore incurred the enmity of constitutional reformers, especially Simon de Montfort.

    (3) Their financial value shown

    1188. *a.* By the fact that the Jews were required to pay £60,000 towards the Saladin Tithe, while the amount due from the whole country was £70,000.

    1255. *β.* Richard of Cornwall accepted the Jews as adequate security for the heavy loans he had made to Henry III.

    (4) They gained special privileges owing to their relation to the King.

        a. They were exempted from ordinary taxation.

        β. Richard I established a special Exchequer Court to receive payments from the Jews, and the Justices of this court took civil cases affecting Jews.

II. Their unpopularity was due to

A. The special privileges they enjoyed.

B. The heavy interest they exacted for loans and the jealousy of wealthy Christians who were forbidden by the Church to lend money at interest.

C. The great profits they made by lending money, to Crusaders in particular.

D. Religious antipathy and the strong opposition of the Church. Grossetête, Bishop of Lincoln, a strong opponent of the Jews.

E. This hatred shown by

(1) **1189.** A general massacre of Jews at Lynn, Norwich, Lincoln, and especially at York, where five hundred having slain their wives and daughters set fire to the castle where they had taken refuge and were burned to death.

(2) **1215.** Magna Carta limited the rights of Jews over their debtors and provided that debts due to Jews should bear no interest during the minority of the deceased debtor's heir and should not be paid out of the widow's dower.

III. The Expulsion of the Jews, 1290.

Edward I, like his mother Eleanor of Provence, was the enemy of the Jews and

A. **1275.**   By the Statute de la Jewerie

(1) Ordered every Jew of twelve and upwards to pay a tax of threepence a year to the King.

(2) Forbade them to lend money at usury.

B. **1290.**   King Edward expelled the Jews from England.

(1) This action was due to his own enmity, to the general hatred of the Jews and to the strong opposition of the Church.   One reason given was because, owing to losses caused by the statute against usury, they had gained illegal profit by clipping the coinage.

(2) The clergy granted the King a tenth of clerical incomes in addition to a general grant of one-fifteenth of movable property made by clergy and laity.   But the King's financial position was greatly weakened by the departure of the Jews, which was partly responsible for the financial crisis of **1294.**

(3) The Jews were allowed to take their money with them. About 16,000 left the country, many of whom, in spite of a safe-conduct granted by the King, were robbed and very cruelly treated as they went.

(4) Italian bankers (especially the Friscobaldi of Florence) took the place of the Jews as the King's agents and incurred similar unpopularity.

References :

A. Medley's *English Constitutional History*, pp. 532–4.

B. *Handbook to Yorkshire*, John Murray, pp. 68–9.

EDWARD I

I. His Work.

A. In England—his work successful.

(1) He carried on the work of Henry II by asserting the royal supremacy over the Church and barons, and abolished the importance of tenure as an element in politics.

(2) He recognised the importance of the people, and his Great and Model Parliament gave national self-government. In 1297 he issued an address to the nation justifying his policy against the complaints of the earls.

(3) His reign was a period of definition. He attempted (e.g. by the distraint of knighthood, the Statute of Westminster, and the recognition of estates in the Model Parliament) to define the functions of every part of the State.

(4) A great legislator, called "the English Justinian." The early part of his reign to 1290 was a great period of constructive legislation, but later legislation was limited by foreign wars and baronial opposition.

B. In Great Britain—his work partially successful.

Edward attempted to unite Great Britain into one kingdom. His design was statesmanlike but premature. His attempt to make Scotland subordinate failed, but he conquered Wales

C. Abroad—his work generally unsuccessful.

(1) He aimed at keeping the Balance of Power in Europe, thus anticipating the policy of Wolsey. But he failed owing to

α. The limited resources at his disposal and the heavy debts his father left ;

β. The wars with Wales and Scotland, which prevented him from using all the resources of England to promote his aims on the Continent.

(2) He succeeded in regaining Gascony 1303, but this was due more to the difficulties in which Philip was placed owing to his quarrels with Boniface VIII and with the Flemings than to the power of England.

II. His Character.

A. Edward I was a man of high aims, of moral life and deep religious feeling.

B. His power of government and organisation had been developed owing to the active part he took in politics during the end of his father's reign, and he showed himself a practical statesman.

C. He generally "kept troth," but at times showed a disposition to respect the letter rather than the spirit of his promises. In the negotiations respecting the succession to the Scottish crown he misused the advantage of his position to assert rights to which he had no claim, and in 1305 he obtained a bull from Clement V to release him from the oath he had sworn in 1301 to keep the Forest Charters.

D. He was generally self-restrained, but his absolute conviction of the justice of his aims made him intolerant of opposition and sometimes violent and vindictive.

E. But he was one of the best men and best kings that have ruled over England.

References :

A. Stubbs' *Constitutional History*, Vol. II, pp. 104–5.

"Edward I." *Twelve English Statesmen*, chap. I.

THOMAS EARL OF LANCASTER

I. His Personal Influence.

Son of Edmund Crouchback, therefore grandson of Henry III, and first cousin to King Edward II. Earl of Lancaster, Leicester, and Derby. He married the daughter of Henry of Lincoln, and thus got the earldoms of Lincoln and Salisbury. Brother-in-law of Philip the Fair and uncle of Queen Isabella.

II. Leader of the Opposition.

Owing to his personal animosity to Gaveston he opposed Edward II, and became the centre of general discontent.

A. Lancaster was the leader of the Ordainers and was largely responsible for the Ordinances of 1311.

(1) The Ordinances provided

α. That illegal exactions should be abolished and the King should "live of his own";

β. That the consent of the baronage was necessary for

1. Alienation of the crown lands,

2. The appointment of the chief officials of the kingdom,

3. The departure of the King from England,

4. The summoning of forces and declaration of war;

γ. That Gaveston and the King's foreign agents (especially the Friscobaldi) should be expelled from the kingdom, and that the customs reserved to the King should be collected by native agents;

δ. That the Charters should be properly observed;

ε. That the privileges of the Church should be maintained;

ζ. That Parliament should meet annually.

(2) Criticism of the Ordinances.

    a. The Petition of 1310, which led to the appointment of the Ordainers (a commission of reform), came from the magnates, and the commons had no voice in the election of the Ordainers. This arrangement followed the precedent of the Mad Parliament, not of Edward I, and was reactionary in character.

    β. The extensive powers claimed for the barons were contrary to the spirit of the constitution, and, if carried out, would probably have led to the establishment of a baronial oligarchy.

    γ. The provisions for the abolition of new taxes show the importance of the work of Edward I's Parliaments.

Thus (δ) the Ordinances do not show an advance in constitutional theory over the Provisions of Oxford, and as a statesman Thomas of Lancaster was behind the time.

B. He was responsible for the murder of Gaveston (who had been recalled and restored to his estates by Edward) at Blacklow Hill, near Warwick, in 1312. Hence the breach between Pembroke and Warrenne (who had promised Gaveston safety), and Lancaster.

III. Ruler of the Country.

A. The deaths of the Earl of Lincoln, Winchelsey in 1313, Gloucester (at Bannockburn), and the discredit of the royal power after Bannockburn, 1314, made Thomas of Lancaster the ruler of the country.

(1) He became the leader of the Council and commander of the army (Pembroke was superseded).

(2) The barons of north supported him.

(3) The commons looked on him as their champion against the bad government of the King.

(4) The clergy looked on him as the supporter of orthodoxy.

B. A bad ruler. No practical policy. Failed to appreciate his duty to cease from opposition and to give good government. Failed to see the constitutional importance of the people, called few parliaments, effected no great reform, and failed to check the growing power of Bruce.

C. Growth of a middle party (Pembroke, Warrenne, and Badlesmere) distinct from the baronial party of Lancaster and the court party of the King. The middle party with the support of the King, and of those desiring strong successful rule, deprived Lancaster of the chief power by the Treaty of Leek in 1318.

D. Growth of a court party, led by the Despensers, who strongly opposed the supremacy of the baronage which Lancaster wished to establish, and, while sympathising with constitutional development, looked to the King as the supreme power.

Hence union of Lancaster and the middle party and banishment of the Despensers. The Queen was refused admission to Leeds, Badlesmere's castle in Kent. The King attacked Badlesmere, Lancaster remaining inactive through hatred of Badlesmere.

1322. Lancaster defeated at Boroughbridge and executed at Pontefract.

IV. The Importance of Lancaster.

A. Lancaster's private character bad. An example of a selfish feudal baron, with no appreciation of constitutional development and of the importance of the Commons. But regarded (wrongly) as a hero by many owing to his opposition to the King.

B. From the struggle of Lancaster and the King arose the blood feuds which led ultimately to the Wars of the Roses.

C. Reaction after the death of Lancaster shown by the assertion at York in 1322: "Matters touching the realm to be established in Parliament by the King and by the consent of the prelates, earls, barons, and *the commonalty of the realm*, as has been hitherto accustomed."

References :

A. Stubbs' *Constitutional History*, Vol. II, pp. 336–68.

B. *The Days of Bruce*, by Aguilar, Warne.

THE CAUSES
OF THE HUNDRED YEARS' WAR

I. Philip VI (Philip of Valois) rightly continued the policy of absorbing the great fiefs, which was essential for the development of a strong monarchy in France. Edward III wished to keep all that was left to England in Guienne and Gascony.

    Therefore the war was inevitable. Other causes are secondary.

II. Philip VI, like his predecessors, strengthened his position by helping the Scots against Edward III, who was thus hampered in his attempt to maintain and extend his possessions in Gascony and Guienne. Therefore Philip gave support and shelter to David Bruce. Hence David's invasion of England which was checked at Neville's Cross 1346.

III. Edward strengthened his position by his alliance with the Emperor Louis of Bavaria, his brother-in-law, 1338. Therefore Benedict XII, in exile at Avignon, the enemy of Louis, stirred up Philip against Edward and the Emperor.

IV. Edward gave shelter to Robert of Artois, Philip's brother-in-law, who claimed the county of Artois. The personal relations between Philip and Edward had been distinctly friendly hitherto, and this fact delayed the beginning of the war. The reception of Robert put an end to these friendly relations.

V. Philip supported Count Louis of Flanders in his struggle against the Flemings, who were routed at Cassel 1328, and ordered the imprisonment of all the English in Flanders. Therefore Edward prohibited the export of English wool, which was indispensable to Flanders as the raw material of the cloth trade. The Flemings, led by Jacob van Artevelde of Ghent, who "showed them that they could not live without the King of England," made an alliance with Edward. The English, who cared little for Scotland and Guienne, resented the injury caused by Philip's policy to English trade and supported Edward. The interference with English trade made the dispute with France a national question.

VI. The Flemings had sworn an oath of allegiance to the King of France, and they felt bound by their oath to obey the King of France. Therefore Edward renewed in 1337 a claim to the French throne which he had made in 1327 and thus secured their allegiance.

A. The reason for his claim to the throne was to secure the allegiance of the Flemings, and the claim was not made until the Flemish question arose. Thus Edward's claim to the throne of France was not (as is sometimes stated) the main cause of the war.

B. The claim that a woman might transmit the right of succession was regarded as reasonable at the time, and such transmission often took place in France in the case of fiefs. The Salic Law was a legal fiction of the next generation, but even so Charles of Navarre, grandson of Louis X, had a better claim than Edward.

C. But the French barons in 1328 had consulted the best interests of France by choosing as king Philip of Valois, a Frenchman born and bred, whose interests were solely French.

VII. The war was supported in England by various classes—

A. The clergy, who strongly resented the dependence of the Pope (Benedict XII) on the French King, owing to the Babylonish captivity at Avignon (1305–1377).

B. The merchants, owing to the interruption with the Flemish trade, the damage done to English shipping by French privateers in the Channel, and the wish to maintain trade with Gascony. The necessity of protecting commerce was recognised by Edward, and partly explains his active naval policy and his attempt to keep command of the narrow seas.

C. The barons and military class, who welcomed the chance of fame and plunder.

Reference :

A. *Political History of England, 1216 – 1277*, by Tout, Longmans, pp. 323–38.

THE HUNDRED YEARS' WAR TO 1375

I. First Period of the War, 1337–1340.

A. The First Confederacy against France.

1338. Attempt of Edward III to unite the Emperor Louis the Bavarian, the Duke of Brabant, the Counts of Guelders and Hainault, and the Flemish towns against Philip.

1338. Louis appointed Edward his Vicar-General west of the Rhine.

1339. Unsuccessful invasion of France. The Emperor and the Flemings gave little assistance. Failure of the first confederacy.

B. The Second Confederacy against France.

1339. Second confederacy formed by Edward, including the Flemings, led by van Artevelde of Ghent and the Duke of Brabant.

1340. Great naval victory at Sluys due to the skill of the English archers. Edward was thus enabled to invade France again, but he failed to capture St. Omer and Tournai.

A truce was made between Edward and Philip, which continued until 1342, owing to Edward's inability to raise money to meet the expense of continuing the war.

Failure of the second confederacy. But the Flemings had profited by the alliance with Edward to weaken the power of the Count of Flanders and to organise their communes.

II. The Succession in Brittany.

Rivalry of John de Montfort, supported by the Celtic population, and Charles of Blois, nephew of Philip VI, for the Duchy of Brittany.

1342. Great victory of the Earl of Northampton, supporting Montfort, at Morlaix.

1345. Edward planned a threefold attack on France from Guienne, Brittany, and Flanders. His advance checked by the murder of van Artevelde, the death of John de Montfort and of Edward's brother-in-law, the Duke of Holland.

III. Creçy, 1346.

A. Successes of the French under John of Normandy (afterwards King John) in Guienne. Edward set out with a large army for Bordeaux, but, partly owing to storms, landed in Normandy, marched along the Seine towards Paris, and retreated towards Picardy to join the Flemings. He crossed the Seine and the Somme (at the ford of Blanche Taque) and defeated Philip at Creçy, near Abbeville.

B. The battle, August 26th, 1346.

(1) The English fought on foot in three battalions commanded by the young Prince of Wales, by the Earls of Northampton and Arundel, and, a reserve force, by the King. Archers were posted on each side of the two former. The English position was strengthened by shallow holes dug along the front of the lines. Edward's forces who had rested the previous night did very little marching on the day of the battle.

(2) The French nobles compelled Philip (who utterly failed as a general) to attack the English, although their main army had not yet come up and their men were tired out with a long day's march and had the sun in their eyes. The shafts of the Genoese crossbowmen, whose strings were wetted by rain, failed to reach the English, whose longbows did great execution. The French men-at-arms rode down the Genoese, but failed to reach the English lines. Fifteen charges made by the French were all unsuccessful, although the Prince of Wales—the hero of the day—was at one time very hard pressed. The French were utterly undisciplined, but fought with great bravery. The French were completely routed, and lost the blind King John of Bohemia, nearly a hundred nobles, 1000 knights, and from 15,000 to 20,000 men. The English lost less than 1000 men.

(3) The tactics of the battle are of great importance.

> α. "It was a combat of infantry against cavalry, of missile weapons against heavy armour and lances, of trained professional soldiers against a combination of foreign mercenaries with disorderly feudal levies." [Lodge, *Close of the Middle Ages.*]

> β. The English archers won the day, and the success of the English archers, mixed with footmen, led to the elimination of the armed knight as a factor in mediæval warfare.

(4) The political results of the battle.

1347. α. Edward III captured Calais, which he made an English town. For two hundred years Calais afforded the English an easy entrance into France.

> β. John of Normandy was compelled to abandon his operations in Guienne, which was reconquered by Henry (formerly Earl, now created Duke of Lancaster), who overran Poitou and sacked Poitiers.

> γ. The French could no longer send effective aid to Charles of Blois in Brittany, where Thomas Dagworth routed and captured Charles at La Roche and ensured the supremacy of Montfort.

(5) 1346. David of Scotland, who had tried to help the French by invading the north of England, was defeated and captured at Neville's Cross, near Durham, by the northern levies.

(6) 1347. The Truce of Calais gave peace for a time to England, France, Scotland, and Brittany. Edward was compelled to make a truce owing to lack of money to carry on the war and to the failure of the Flemings and the great nobles of the Netherlands to render effective help. In attempting to conquer France he was undertaking a task too great for his resources, although the glory gained at Creçy obscured the fact.

IV. **From Creçy to Poitiers.**

A. Brittany.

Gradual success of the French party under Bertrand du Guesclin partly because Edward III could not send adequate reinforcements.

B. Ponthieu.

Gradual extension of English power around Calais.

C. **1350.** Great naval victory over Spanish privateers off Winchelsea. "Espagnols sur Mer."

D. Guienne.

(1) **1355.** Unsuccessful attempt to co-operate with Charles the Bad, King of Navarre, whose lands in Normandy afforded a means of attacking France from the north-west.

(2) **1355.** Expedition of the Black Prince to Narbonne, and devastation of French territory adjoining Guienne.

[(3) **1356.** Berwick, recently captured by the Scotch, recaptured by Edward III.]

E. The Battle of Poitiers, **1356.**

(1) **1356.** Expedition of Henry Duke of Lancaster to Normandy to help Charles the Bad.

Northward march of the Black Prince to join Lancaster on the Loire. The Prince intercepted by King John at Poitiers.

(2) The battle, September 19th, **1356.**

α. The French had 40,000[1] men, the English 7000.

β. The English were drawn up in three "battles," two in front, under Suffolk and Salisbury, and Oxford and Warwick, and one in the rear under the Black Prince.

γ. The English position was well chosen on higher ground than that held by the French. The left flank was protected by the River Miausson, the front by a hedge, a ditch and bushes and vineyards affording cover to the archers. Thus the advantage of superior numbers enjoyed by the French was somewhat diminished.

---

[1] Froissart gives rather different numbers engaged at Creçy (page 166) and Poitiers. See *Froissart's Creçy and Poitiers*, Blackie.

δ. The French fought mainly on foot and the battle was stubbornly contested. The English victory was due to the skill of the archers, the difficulty the French found in delivering an attack owing to the narrowness of the lane leading up to the English front, the timely help brought by the Black Prince to the two leading "battles" when hard pressed by King John, and a successful attack made on the French flank by a small force of cavalry led by the Captal de Buch, a Gascon nobleman. King John and his son Philip (afterwards Philip the Bold of Burgundy) were captured, and the French lost heavily, but, as at Creçy, the English were too weak to follow up their victory.

V. **The Treaty of Bretigny, 1360. "The Great Peace."**

A. France was now in a miserable condition owing to the war, to gross mismanagement of the finances, to a rising of the people of Paris against the Dauphin[1] Charles, who was acting as Regent during his father's imprison ment in London, to the Jacquerie,[2] a rising of the peasants against the nobles, and to the ravages of the bands of soldiers called the Free Companies.

B. But the French refused to confirm the terms made by King John in London, and in 1359 Edward again invaded France. The French declined to fight pitched battles, and Edward, finding it most difficult to get food for his army, agreed to the Treaty of Bretigny.

C. The Treaty.

   (1) Edward gave up his claims to the French Crown, and to the Angevin dominions north of the Loire.

   (2) Edward received as absolute owner, and without any obligation of homage, Calais, Ponthieu, Guines in the north, and Guienne, Gascony, Poitou, and Saintonge in the south.

[1] The eldest son of the King of France was called "the Dauphin," because he was invested with Dauphiné in the east of France.

[2] So called from "Jacques Bonhomme," the nickname of the peasants.

(3) King John to be ransomed for 3,000,000 crowns. This treaty was not a final settlement. The growing national feeling of France and the inadequate resources of England made the ultimate recovery of the ceded territory certain.

VI. From the Treaty of Bretigny to the End of Edward III's Reign.

A. Brittany.

1364. The war of the Breton succession ended with the defeat of the French under Bertrand du Guesclin at Aurai by Sir John Chandos and the recognition as Duke of Brittany of Montfort, who did homage to Charles V of France.

B. Aquitaine.

(1) 1367. The Black Prince, now Duke of Aquitaine, by a victory at Najara, restored Pedro the Cruel to the throne of Castile, from which he had been driven by his brother Henry of Trastamara, aided by Bertrand du Guesclin. But the English forces were greatly weakened by pestilence, the health of the Black Prince was ruined, and he was greatly embarrassed by the refusal of Pedro to pay his share of the expenses.

(2) The Black Prince was a good governor, and the towns of Aquitaine flourished under his rule. But the barons were jealous of the English officials, and a hearth tax imposed to meet the expenses of the campaign of 1367 roused great opposition. They appealed to Charles V, and war was renewed.

(3) 1370. Limoges was recaptured from the French by the Black Prince. Massacre of the inhabitants—men, women, and children. The great blot on the reputation of the Black Prince.

C. The ruin of the English power.

> **1372.** Henry of Trastamara (who had slain his brother Pedro and held Castile in defiance of John of Gaunt, who had married Pedro's daughter) defeated the English fleet under the Earl of Pembroke at La Rochelle. The English thus lost the command of the sea gained by the victories of Sluys, **1340,** and " Espagnols sur Mer," **1350.**

> **1373.** John of Gaunt, obliged to march overland owing to the defeat of the fleet, led a vast army from Calais through Central France to Bordeaux. Great English loss, owing to the tactics of Du Guesclin, who continually harassed the army, but declined a pitched battle.
>
> Gradual loss of Southern France.

> **1375.** The truce of Bruges ended the fighting in Edward III's reign.
>
> The English lost all their conquests, except Bordeaux, Bayonne, Calais, and Ponthieu ; but these gave the English facilities for invading France, which they used with success later.

D. The causes of the English failure.

> (1) Charles V was not a mere knight-errant like John, but diplomatic, patient. He re-established the Government, united France, and aroused French national feeling.

> (2) England had no foreign allies.

>> α. Pedro was dead, and Henry of Trastamara hostile.
>>
>> β. Charles the Bad of Navarre joined the French.
>>
>> γ. The marriage of Philip of Burgundy (brother of Charles V) with Margaret of Flanders strengthened the influence of France in the Netherlands.
>>
>> δ. The Holy Roman Emperor Wenceslaus was hostile to Edward.

ccesses of Bertrand du Guesclin and the
ion of guerilla warfare by the French. John
Gaunt in 1373 found no enemy to defeat in battle,
and could not capture towns.

The loss of the command of the sea and the consequent difficulty of sending reinforcements.

(5) Unrest in Aquitaine.

(6) The ruined health of Edward III and the Black Prince.

(7) Dissatisfaction in England at the want of military success and consequent reluctance of Parliament to grant supplies.

References :

A. *The Close of the Middle Ages*, by Lodge, Rivingtons, chap. IV.
"Creçy." *Art of War in the Middle Ages*, by Oman, pp. 603–15.
"Poitiers." *Art of War in the Middle Ages*, pp. 623–34.

C. *Sir Nigel* and *The White Company*, by Conan Doyle.

THE BLACK DEATH

I. Origin and Course.

It came from China; appeared in Europe first at Constantinople, and followed the trade routes; 1348, first appeared in England at Weymouth, then in Bristol, London, East Anglia, and Lancashire; and then Scotland. It reappeared in 1361 and 1369.

It destroyed one-third, some say one-half, of the population. "In Bristol the living could hardly bury the dead," and two hundred were buried daily in Charterhouse Yard, London, in 1348–1349. The old escaped better than the young, and labourers and clergy died in great numbers. Parishes were depopulated; districts thrown out of cultivation; cattle and sheep exterminated.

II. **Results.**

A. Labourers.

(1) Some landlords had commuted for money payment [i.e. for rent] the services their tenants formerly rendered. The labourers, owing to the diminution in their numbers caused by the Black Death, demanded higher wages. The landlords now tried to exact the old services from their tenants instead of rent, and to limit the wages paid to labourers.

(2) Statutes of Labourers, **1349** and **1351**.

α. Compelled landlords to pay and labourers to accept the rate of wages current before the Black Death.

β. Prohibited labourers from changing their residence or breaking contracts.

γ. Prohibited a rise in the price of goods.

1. These statutes were not simple tyranny on the part of Parliament in favour of landlords, because the fixing of prices helped the poor, and it was thought in the Middle Ages that prices and wages could properly be fixed by law.

2. These laws were not generally carried out, but the attempt to enforce them led to bitter class feeling. The labourers often got higher wages. Gradually the old services were swept away, and the relation of landlord and tenant was substituted for ineffective feudal tenure.

Thus arose the social difference between landlord and tenant which was one of the causes of the Peasants' Revolt.

B. Landlords.

They suffered much from the change, especially ecclesiastical landlords, who were heavily taxed. The monks, owing to the fall in their rents, were greatly impoverished and never quite recovered their former position. But now began the policy of turning lands into sheep farms instead of arable land, and grazing proved more profitable than agriculture. "The profit of the fleece was greater than the profit of the plough."

C. Clergy.

The diminution in the numbers of the clergy led to demands for higher payment. Non-residence and neglect of cures followed. The newly ordained clergy were often badly educated.

Therefore the bishops ordered the clergy to be content with previous payments. To meet the demand for additional clergy new religious houses were founded (e.g. Charterhouse by Sir Walter Manny), and several colleges were now established at Oxford and Cambridge to train secular priests.

D. The King.

It was difficult to raise taxes from landowners owing to their losses. The mortality of sheep affected the royal revenues because the King depended largely on wool as a source of income.

III. General Results.

In spite of the very important results of the Black Death it is incorrect to regard it as "the one great turning point in the social and economic history of England."

A. The Black Death was not an isolated phenomenon, and the same effects were not found in other countries where it appeared.

B. It is very important because it accelerated changes which had already begun in England, not because it started new movements.

References :

A. *Social England*, Vol. II, chap. VI.

C. *The Gathering of Brother Hilarius*, by Fairless, Murray.

THE GOOD PARLIAMENT, 1376

I. **Position of the Commons.**

    A. The Commons had been separated from the Lords 1341, and gained strength owing to the union of the knights of the shire—socially connected with the great barons—with the burgesses.

    B. Increase of power of the Commons during this century, e.g. Petitions of Commons which had received royal assent to be made into statutes without change, 1341.

    C. But they did not for some time claim supervision over the whole of the administration, e.g. in 1348 they refused to advise the King as to the Hundred Years' War " because they were so ignorant and simple."

II. **Popular feeling roused by**

    A. The failures of the French war.

        (1) 1372. Defeat of the fleet at Rochelle and loss of command of the sea.

        (2) Utter failure of John of Gaunt's expedition.

        (3) Loss of Guienne (except Bordeaux and Bayonne) owing to the successes of Bertrand du Guesclin.

    B. The action of John of Gaunt, "whose doings were ever contrary"; who, relying upon the assistance of Alice Perrers, the King's mistress, and of Lords Neville of Raby (Steward), Latimer (Treasurer), and Richard Lyons (Edward III's agent), controlled the Government, which the King, through age and weakness, could not direct. He was suspected of aiming at the succession.

III. **The Good Parliament.**

    A. Strong action of the Commons in the Good Parliament 1376. The first time the Commons had become the champions of national rights. But the leading part was taken by the knights of the shire, not the burgesses. The Commons supported by

(1) The Black Prince, anxious to ensure the succession of his son Richard,

(2) Edmund Mortimer, Earl of March, husband of Philippa of Clarence and father of Roger Mortimer, the next heir after Richard,

(3) William of Wykeham and Courtenay Bishop of London, the leaders of the clerical party, whom John of Gaunt bitterly attacked.

B. Action of the Good Parliament.

Peter de la Mare, steward of the Earl of March, appointed Speaker. The first man to exercise the full functions of this office.

(1) The Commons Impeached[1] Latimer for malversation and treachery, and Lyons, who had used his opportunities to manipulate trade.

Attacked Alice Perrers, who had sat on the judges' seat in the Courts at Westminster, for interference with justice.

Latimer and Lyons imprisoned and fined. Alice Perrars banished from court.

(2) Protested against Papal exactions, mismanagement of the war, and arbitrary taxation.

(3) Demanded annual Parliaments, free elections of knights of the shire without interference from the crown, and the enforcement of the Statutes of Labourers.

(4) On the death of the Black Prince petitioned for the recognition of Richard II as heir to the throne, and frustrated the attempt of John of Gaunt to nullify the right of succession through a woman, and thus to abrogate the claim of Roger Mortimer.

(5) Petitioned for the appointment of twelve councillors to "enforce the royal council." This petition was granted by the King.

[1] Impeachment is an accusation " by the Commons, sitting as a Grand Jury of the whole nation," before the House of Lords, as "a High Criminal Court of State."

IV. **On the Dissolution of Parliament its work was annulled by John of Gaunt.**

> The newly appointed councillors were dismissed. Latimer, Lyons, and Alice Perrers, were recalled, and Peter de la Mare imprisoned. The possessions of William of Wykeham were seized, and an alliance made between John of Gaunt and Wycliffe in an attack on the power and wealth of the Church.

V. **The importance of the Good Parliament.**

A. The Commons took the lead in national policy for the first time and claimed the right of Parliament to control the whole administration

B. The first use of Impeachment. A powerful weapon against ministers, later used against the Earl of Suffolk **1386**, Duke of Suffolk **1450**, Mompesson (for fraud) in **1621**, Buckingham for failure to guard the high seas and lending ships to be used against the Huguenots **1626**, Strafford (changed to a Bill of Attainder) **1640**, Laud for high treason **1641**, Clarendon **1667**, Sacheverell for teaching the doctrine of passive obedience **1710**, Warren Hastings for misgovernment in India **1788**.

C. Assertion of the responsibility of ministers to Parliament.

Reference :

A. Stubbs' *Constitutional History*, Vol. II, pp. 448–58.

ENGLAND AND THE PAPACY IN THE FOURTEENTH CENTURY

I. **Steady growth of National Opposition to the Pope.**

A. Resistance to Papal demands for money.

(1) The Good Parliament protested against payments to Rome, and said that five times as much money was paid to the Pope as to the King.

(2) Repeated refusal of Parliament to pay the arrears of John's tribute claimed by the Popes.

N

(3) The clergy, heavily taxed for war, became impatient of Papal demands for first fruits, and objected

    α. To the drain of coin from England ;

    β. To supplying money to pay the expenses of the "French Popes" at Avignon.

B. Resistance to the "provision" by the Pope of foreign clergymen for English livings.

    1351. The Statute of Provisors was passed to prevent the Pope from presenting foreigners to English livings. Foreign clergy were unpopular because

        α. They were often ignorant of English.

        β. They were generally non-resident.

        γ. They led to the withdrawal of money from England to the Continent.

C. Resistance to the Papal claim of authority over English law courts. Hence the Statutes of Præmunire.

    (1) 1353. The First Statute of Præmunire

        Forbade suits cognisable in the King's courts to be referred to any foreign court on pain of outlawry.

        This statute was aimed at the Papal courts, but they were not specially named.

    (2) 1393. The Great Statute of Præmunire.

        Any one obtaining bulls or other legal instruments from Rome to forfeit his goods.

D. The authority of the Papacy was much impaired,

    (1) By the "Babylonish Captivity" of the Popes at Avignon **1305–1377.** The Avignonese Popes were Frenchmen, under the influence of the kings of France and regarded as allies of France. Hence the refusal of Edward III to accept, during the Hundred Years' War, the mediation of Benedict XII and Clement VI and the hostility in England to the "French Popes."

(2) By the Great Schism, **1378–1417,** during which rival Popes claimed the Papacy.

Great indignation was aroused in England at Bishop Despenser's "Crusade" in Flanders, **1383,** to support the Flemings (the adherents of the orthodox Urban VI) against Charles V of France (an adherent of the Antipope Clement VII).

E. Growth in England of national sentiment, stimulated by the Hundred Years' War and by the growth of vernacular literature, especially Wycliffe's translation of the Bible and Chaucer's poems. This national sentiment strengthened opposition to foreign domination.

II. Growth of Opposition in England to the Clergy.

A. The privileges of the clergy were annulled or diminished.

(1) The clergy were compelled to appear when summoned before a civil court.

(2) Failure of Boniface VIII to save them from royal taxation by the bull Clericis Laicos **1296.**

B. Growing feeling against the wealth and luxury of the clergy (shown in *Piers Plowman* and the Prologue to the *Canterbury Tales*) and the employment of clergy in secular work.

III. John Wycliffe, "the Morning Star of the Reformation," about 1320–1384.

A. Born in North Yorkshire, became Warden of Balliol Hall at Oxford, about **1360,** and Professor of Divinity. Appointed ambassador at Bruges **1374,** and during his residence abroad was profoundly impressed by the abuses of the Roman Catholic Church.

B. He represented the national feeling of opposition to the Pope and clergy.

(1) He asserted that "dominion was founded in grace," i.e. that no one could rightly exercise authority unless he was a good man. He taught that clergy should exercise "ecclesiastical dominion" over the lives of men, but should not accept secular employment.

(2) He attacked the higher clergy for their immorality and wealth, and preached the doctrine of apostolic poverty against the "possessioner monks," who had large estates. He advocated the disendowment of the Church, and asserted the right of the Crown to seize the temporal possessions of the Church.

(3) He opposed Papal provisions and payments to the Pope.

(4) He was at first orthodox in doctrine, although he attacked clerical abuses, and among his strongest supporters were the Mendicant Friars, whose vows bound them to poverty.

(5) John of Gaunt strongly opposed William of Wykeham and the higher clergy and, although caring nothing for the reform of morals, supported Wycliffe's attack on the wealth of the Church.

C. Wycliffe's change in doctrine.

(1) 1377. Convocation, largely through enmity towards John of Gaunt, summoned Wycliffe for trial by bishops at St. Paul's. The trial was broken up by Gaunt's supporters. Gaunt's palace, the Savoy, was pillaged by a London mob owing to insults offered by his followers to Courtenay Bishop of London.

(2) Wycliffe's rejection of Transubstantiation.

α. His argument was at first logical. Accidents (i.e. qualities) cannot exist in the abstract, but involve substance. The qualities of bread and wine continue in the sacred emblems, and the substance must therefore be bread and wine, not the Body and Blood of Christ.

1379 or 1380. β. Following St. Augustine he taught that "Christians receive the Lord's body spiritually."

γ. The rejection of Transubstantiation was "the turning point in Wycliffe's career." John of Gaunt remained orthodox and forsook Wycliffe, but " Good Queen Anne," Anne of Bohemia, who had married Richard II in 1382, supported him, and Lollardy gained strength at court.

D. 1380. Wycliffe began to translate the Bible into English.

    a. He declared that Scripture afforded a sufficient guide for conduct, and that a godly life, based on the teaching of Christ, was more important than Sacraments. The Church consisted of all who had been saved through Christ, and not of the clergy alone.

    β. Wycliffe "the founder of English prose."

E. 1381 (about). Organised his " Poor Preachers," mostly Oxford men, whose learning, piety, and simple life offered a strong contrast to the immorality, laziness, and growing wealth of the friars, who had now become strong opponents of Wycliffe.

F. The Peasants' Revolt, 1381.

    The Peasants' Revolt, though not a religious movement, affected Wycliffe.

    (1) The Socialism of the Peasants' Revolt was confused with Wycliffe's assertion of apostolic poverty and of the equality of all men before God, and Lollardism was somewhat discredited in consequence.

    (2) Wycliffe's strong opponent, Courtenay Bishop of London, became archbishop on the murder of Archbishop Sudbury by the peasants, and in **1382** summoned a council at Blackfriars [called " the council of the earthquake,'' because disturbed by a shock], in which Wycliffe was condemned as a heretic owing to

        a. His denial of Transubstantiation ;

        β. His rejection of auricular confession.

G. Wycliffe retired to Lutterworth, where he died of a stroke of paralysis received while he was saying Mass, **1384.**

    His followers (called Lollards, possibly from "lullen," to sing) were expelled from Oxford by Courtenay, but suffered little persecution under Richard II. They were crushed in the fifteenth century, largely owing to Henry IV's desire to secure the support of the Church, and the literary and intellectual barrenness of that century is partly due to the consequent loss of freedom of thought and expression

References :

A. *Historical Essays and Reviews,* by Creighton, Longmans, " John Wycliffe."

Social England, Vol. II, pp. 214–34.

PEASANTS' REVOLT, 1381

gricultural.

(1) Discontent caused by the attempts of the landlords to enforce the Statutes of Labourers and by the desire of the labourers to take advantage of the increased demand for labour and of the rise in wages caused by the Black Death.

(2) The labourers were harassed by petty demands (dues on sales, special payment to landlords at festivals, restrictions on hunting rabbits—a rabbit on a pole one of the emblems of the rebels), and also by cruel punishments, e.g. branding for breaches of the Statute of Labourers. Hence

    a. Attacks on monasteries. The monks had insisted on their rights as landlords, and the teaching of Wycliffe had roused strong feeling against the clergy.

    β. Attacks on lawyers, who, by finding faults in deeds of manumission, had enabled landlords to compel many labourers to return to the old conditions. Hence the attack on the Temple in London, the destruction of manor rolls and records, and the murder of lawyers.

B. Political.

(1) Discontent with the conduct of the French war. The failure of John of Gaunt was contrasted with the success of Philpot, a London merchant, who raised a fleet at his own expense and defeated Scotch pirates in 1378. The French were regaining Guienne, had secured the command of the Channel and burnt Gravesend in 1380.

(2) Imposition of taxes to meet expenses of the war.

1379. A graduated poll-tax failed to produce as much as was needed.

1380. Therefore a poll-tax of three groats per head was imposed "on every lay person in the realm save beggars." This was unfair and pressed very heavily on the poorest classes, hitherto exempt from taxation.

The poll-tax was the immediate cause of the revolt.

C. In the towns.

Very varied causes.

(1) To win privileges from landlords, e.g. at St. Albans where the Abbey claimed great authority.

(2) The desire of the poorer classes to limit the power of a rich oligarchy of merchants, or of journeymen to get higher wages. At Winchester there was a rising of Craftsmen against Merchants.

(3) At Cambridge the resentment of the townspeople at the special privileges of the University.

(4) Hatred of foreigners. Frequent attacks on Flemings and Dutch.

D. A vague Socialism.

The Peasants' Revolt was not directly encouraged by Wycliffe, but the socialistic aspect of it was indirectly encouraged by his doctrine of the equality of men before God and by his attacks on the wealth of the clergy. The preaching of John Ball, "the mad priest of Kent," diffused and to a considerable extent created this feeling. His sermon on Blackheath from the text—

> When Adam delved and Eve span,
> Where was then the gentleman?

E. A general feeling of discontent in the country due to resentment against Papal claims, scorn of the immorality of the nobles, confidence in or opposition to John of Gaunt, the presence of many soldiers and sailors discharged from service and prevented from finding work by the restrictions of the guilds.

Thus while the poll-tax was the immediate cause, it would not by itself have led to the outbreak. "It was the fact that this new grievance came at a moment when ancient social problems had reached boiling point that led to an explosion."

II. The course of the Rising.

A. Essex.

The Revolt first broke out in Essex, where the grievances were agricultural. March of the rebels to Mile End. Their demands were—the abolition of villeinage, rent to be 4d. per acre, liberty to buy and sell in markets.

The peasants met by the King at Mile End. "I am your king and lord; good people, what will ye?"

Richard II did not really sympathise with them, but granted all their demands although he had no constitutional right to do this.

Thirty clerks drew up guarantees of indemnity and the people went home.

B. Kent.

The rising due mainly to political causes. Wat Tyler was probably an Essex man, not connected with Dartford, and the story of the murder of the tax-collector who insulted his daughter is untrue.

The rebels marched on London, and were addressed by John Ball on Blackheath. Great negligence on the part of the authorities responsible for the defence of London. The rebels burned John of Gaunt's palace, the Savoy, but hanged a rebel who stole a cup, thus showing that plunder was not their main object.

Next day they attacked the Tower, and slew Archbishop Sudbury and Hales the Treasurer.

The meeting with the King at Smithfield and death of Tyler. Great bravery of the young King.

"I am your captain and your king. Follow me." A promise of emancipation made by Richard.

C. The Eastern Counties.

(1) Norfolk.

Led by a dyer named John Lyster, "the King of the Commons." Captured Yarmouth and murdered Flemish wool merchants, who had settled in East Anglia owing to dissensions in Flanders. Put down by Despenser Bishop of Norwich, "in helm and cuirass, girt with his two-edged sword."

(2) Hertfordshire.

At St. Albans William Grindecobbe led the rebels, who broke to pieces the millstones which had ground the corn that they had to supply to the Abbey mill. This rising was primarily an attempt to restrict the feudal rights of the Abbey.

III. **Results.**

A. An apparent failure. Put down by force. All the leaders and many of their followers executed. Justice Tresillian conducted the assizes. The concessions made by the King were withdrawn on protest of Parliament, and the King's real feelings were shown by his answer to petitioners, " Villeins ye are, and villeins ye shall remain."

B. John of Gaunt, alarmed by the outburst of popular hatred, henceforth supported the Crown, but practically disappears as a political leader.

C. But villeinage gradually died out. The landlords, through fear, granted the demands of the villeins, as many had done before 1381. But the increase in wages led to the extension of grazing and the enclosure of commons for this purpose, and this was one of the causes of later discontent.

References :

A. *The Political History of England, 1377–1485*, chap. II.

C. *Long Will*, by Converse, Longmans, and
Robert Annys, by Meyer, Macmillan.

THE MERCILESS PARLIAMENT, 1388

I. **Events preceding the Merciless Parliament.**

A. The growing importance of the Commons, who claimed the right of appropriating supplies and auditing accounts. They tried to make the King "live of his own," and protested against his gifts to favourites.

This importance was shown in the Good Parliament by the assertion of the right to control taxation and to control the administration.

B. General discontent in the country (shown by the Peasants' Revolt) still continued.

(1) Dissatisfaction about the French war, especially with the failure of Despenser's "crusade" in Flanders (checked at Ypres 1383), and the capture of Ghent —friendly to England—by the French.

The King and Suffolk wanted peace, while the barons' party wanted war.

(2) Dissatisfaction owing to the failure of operations against the Scotch 1385. A French force landed near the Forth. Richard II's expedition to Scotland failed, although Edinburgh was captured, because the Scotch avoided a general engagement.

C. A strong feeling on the part of the barons against the King's favourites :—

Sir Simon Burley, his old tutor.

Sir Nicholas Brember,[1] Lord Mayor of London and head of the "clothing guilds."

Robert de Vere, Earl of Oxford.

Michael de la Pole, Earl of Suffolk.

D. The King's temper bad, he lacked self-restraint and tact.

He struck Archbishop Courtenay for referring to the supposed plot by Richard against John of Gaunt. Angry scenes with Gaunt, who believed that Richard was plotting against his life. Richard refused to work with the Commons, but, relying on the advice of favourites, aimed at strengthening his own power. He refused to rearrange his household at their request. He "would not remove the meanest scullion in his kitchen at their bidding." He made extravagant grants to his favourites, and created de Vere Marquis and Duke of Dublin, with rights over the Pale.

[1] The reliance of Richard II on Brember and de la Pole supports the theory that in his reign we get the beginning of the alliance between the King and the commercial classes against the barons. This alliance, which formed an important element in the policy of the Yorkist and Tudor kings, proved premature in Richard's case.

E. The first attack on Suffolk.

> Led by Gloucester, who compelled Richard to submit by referring to the fate of Edward II.

(1) Suffolk was impeached for corruption, malversation, and failure to relieve Ghent. He made a good defence—he had acted by the King's orders, with the consent of the Council, and had done good service. He was imprisoned.

(2) A Council of Eleven was appointed to govern England and to control the King's household.

(3) The King refused to accept reform, and released Suffolk.

(4) The judges at Nottingham, including Tresillian, told the King that

> α. The sentence on Suffolk was wrong;
>
> β. The appointment of the Council of Eleven was wrong;
>
> γ. The King alone had the right of dismissing ministers;
>
> δ. The King's opponents were traitors.

(5) The King sent de Vere to raise a force in Cheshire, thus incurring the danger of Civil War. Therefore Henry of Derby, son of John of Gaunt, left the King. Vere was routed at Radcot Bridge, in Oxfordshire, and the King was placed at the mercy of the barons.

II. The Merciless Parliament, 1388,

> Packed by Gloucester, and supported by the City of London.

A. The "Lords Appellant."

(1) Derby, Nottingham, Gloucester, Arundel, and Warwick "appealed" the five traitors, for

> α. Using the King for their own purpose, and withdrawing him from the magnates.
>
> β. Making the King waste his treasure.
>
> γ. Treason in favour of France.
> And some foolish accusations.
>
> δ. Vere accused of wishing to become King of Dublin.

ε. Brember accused of wishing to change the name of London to Troynovant.

(2) Execution of Burley, Brember, and Tresillian.

(3) Translation of Archbishop Neville to St. Andrews, a schismatic see which he could not approach owing to the Scotch war.

B. Reward of the Appellants.

Arundel's brother made Archbishop of York.

Gloucester got the lands of de Vere.

The Lords Appellant, although they had protested against the waste of public money, received £20,000.

The Lords Appellant secured the control of the government.

III. Cessation of Strife, 1389.

On the attainment of his majority the King displaced Gloucester and wisely appointed Edward III's old ministers to vacancies on the Council, e.g. William of Wykeham.

John of Gaunt returned after an unsuccessful attempt to gain the throne of Castile and supported the King.

Derby went on a " crusade " with the Knights of the Teutonic Order (who protected the frontier of Germany against the heathen of the Baltic).

"Good Queen Anne" of Bohemia had an excellent influence over Richard II.

Thus the King's position was strengthened and for about eight years he ruled well.

IV. Criticism of the Merciless Parliament.

A. Not a constitutional revolution. The King yielded only owing to fear of the fate of Edward II.

B. Shows the importance of Parliament.

1. The barons acted not by themselves, as in 1311, but through Parliament.

2. The Lords decided that the action of the appellants was legal—though contrary to common law—owing to the sanction of Parliament.

C. Shows that the nobles still retained great power, and the real cause of their action was that Suffolk, who was far superior in character and ability to the favourites of Edward II, prevented them from exercising supreme power during Richard's minority.

Reference :

A. Stubbs' *Constitutional History*, Vol. II, pp. 495–507.

THE REVENGE OF RICHARD II

I. **The King ruled well until 1397 and England had Peace.**

A. The Spanish war ended on the return of John of Gaunt

B. The madness of Charles VI diminished the danger from France.

C. Steady support given to Richard by John of Gaunt, who was invested with the Duchy of Aquitaine.

II. **Richard was probably determined on Vengeance, but he hid his Designs.**

A. Queen Anne died **1394.** Removal of a restraining influence over Richard. Richard struck Arundel in Westminster Abbey at the funeral.

B. Richard married Isabel of France in **1396.** Truce with France.

(1) Isabel was only seven, and therefore there was no hope of an heir for years, and thus Richard's position was weakened.

(2) Probably the absolutism of the French kings encouraged Richard to assert his prerogative.

(3) Condemnation to death of Haxey (who escaped by claiming benefit of clergy) owing to Richard's anger, for protesting in the Commons in **1397** against the number of bishops and ladies at court

C. The isolation of the Appellants.

(1) Arundel was expelled from the Council for attacking John of Gaunt, whose badge Richard wore as a sign of his firm friendship.

Bitter enmity between Arundel and John of Gaunt.

(2) Gloucester was unpopular owing to his factious conduct in the Council.

(3) The King pretended that Gloucester, Warwick, and Arundel had formed a plot against him.

III. The King's Revenge 1397.

A. Eight lords (including Derby and Nottingham, two of the former Lords Appellant) "appealed" Warwick, Glouces-ter, and Arundel.

B. Gloucester died in prison at Calais.

Probably smothered by Richard's orders.

C. Arundel was executed after condemnation in a packed Parlia-ment, in spite of his protest, "The faithful Commons are not here."

D. Warwick banished.

E. Archbishop Arundel translated to Saint Andrews.

F. The estates of the victims divided among the Appellants. New titles granted; five dukes created in one day. Derby and Nottingham made Dukes of Hereford and Norfolk.

IV. The King Absolute.

A. 1397. A packed Parliament. The King's faithful servant, Bussy, became Speaker.

(1) Annulled the Acts of 1388 and the condemnation of Suffolk 1386.

(2) Confirmed the opinions of the judges in favour of the King at Nottingham 1387.

B. 1398. The Shrewsbury Parliament.

1. Made the King independent financially by giving him a subsidy on wool for life.

2. Delegated the powers of Parliament to a council of eighteen.

"A resolute attempt not to evade but to destroy the limitations which for nearly two centuries the nation, first through the baronage alone and latterly through the united Parliament, had been labouring to impose on the King."—Stubbs.

C. Thus the King was absolute, but

1. He owed his position to the action of Parliament.
2. His supporters, called the "Dukelings," lacked the strength of the old feudal nobles.

Reference :

A. Stubbs' *Constitutional History*, Vol. II, pp. 513–25.

THE FALL OF RICHARD

I. Richard had never really forgiven Derby (Hereford) and Nottingham (Norfolk) for their action in 1388. An opportunity of vengeance occurred when Hereford accused Norfolk of urging him to join a plot against Richard II through fear of the King's vengeance. Richard banished Norfolk for life and Hereford for ten years. The heavier punishment of Norfolk suggested belief in his guilt, and in that case the sentence on Hereford was obviously unjust.

II. Richard strengthened his position by maintaining a bodyguard of Cheshire archers, and to meet the cost took forced loans.

III. Richard frightened people by

A. Condemning in 1398 seventeen counties which had supported the Lords Appellant to pay a heavy fine [called *Le Pleasaunce* because the King fixed the amount according to his pleasure],

B. Compelling his enemies to sign blank papers to be filled up as he wished,

C. Ordering sheriffs to report persons speaking ill of the King.

>These measures were not vigorously enforced, but caused much fear.

IV. On the death of John of Gaunt (whose last years afforded a striking contrast to his earlier life, and partly justify Shakespeare's favourable verdict), in 1399, Richard confiscated estates which ought to have gone to Hereford.

V. Roger Earl of March (Richard's cousin and heir), Lord-Lieutenant of Ireland, slain 1398. Richard went to Ireland to put down a rising, and was thus absent when Hereford landed at Ravenspur, nominally to claim his ancestral possessions. Most of his faithful friends accompanied Richard; his uncle, the Duke of York was left as regent, but he was too weak to oppose Hereford, whose design on the crown was facilitated by the death of Roger, a possible rival. Hereford was supported by the Earls of Northumberland and Westmorland and recognised by the Duke of York. Bristol captured by Hereford.

VI. Richard submitted and was deposed by Parliament 30 September, 1399. He was accused of

A. Injustice to Hereford, Arundel, and Gloucester.

B. Breaking the constitution by

1. Corrupting the judges;

2. Delegating the power of Parliament to a council of eighteen;

3. Claiming absolute power, e.g. by saying that the "laws lay in his mouth";

4. Tampering with elections;

5. Interfering with the appointment of sheriffs;

C. Appealing to the Pope—strong anti-Papal feeling in England.

VII. Criticism.

   A. "Richard had challenged the constitution" and tried to stop the course of constitutional development. An unsuccessful attempt to anticipate the policy of the Tudors.

   B. He fell not because of his vengeance in 1397, but because of his foolish policy since 1398, which caused a general feeling of insecurity. "He fooled away the crown." The injustice to Hereford was the occasion, not the sole cause, of his fall.

   C. He made no effort to keep his power. Left at Milford the army which might have saved him.

References :

   A. Stubbs' *Constitutional History*, Vol. II, pp. 525–36.

   B. Shakespeare, *Richard II :*—

      ACT I, *Scene* 3 : "All places that the eye of heaven visits," etc.

      ACT II, *Scene* 1 : "Methinks I am a prophet new inspired," etc.

THE POSITION OF HENRY IV AT HIS ACCESSION

A. His Claim to the Throne.

   (1) He claimed it "by right blood coming from King Henry III." He asserted, wrongly, that Edmund Crouchback, the ancestor of the Lancastrians, was the elder son of Henry III.

   By hereditary right the real heir was Edmund Mortimer, Earl of March, great-great-grandson of Edward III.

   (2) "Through that right that God of His Grace hath sent me with the help of my kin and my friends to recover it."

      i.e. By right of conquest.

o

(3) He owed his crown to conquest sanctioned by election by Parliament. Parliamentary support alone could ensure the continuation of his dynasty; his poverty put him at the mercy of Parliament, which in Henry IV's reign attained a power greater than any predecessor or successor to the time of the Stuarts.

B. **The King's Supporters.**

    (1) The party of the Lords Appellant.

    (2) The Church, which supported the King because of his opposition to the Lollards.

C. **The King's Difficulties.**

    (1) Strong baronial opposition.

        a. Richard II's friends opposed Henry IV, especially his half-brother, John Holland, Earl of Huntingdon (formerly Duke of Exeter), and Thomas Holland, Earl of Kent (formerly Duke of Surrey), a nephew of John Holland. Richard II's existence was a continual danger to Henry, as it afforded a rallying ground for the disaffected.

        β. Many barons supported the hereditary claims of the Earl of March.

        γ. The Percies (Northumberland, Hotspur, and Worcester) had ensured the King's succession, had lent him money, but were dissatisfied with their rewards and very turbulent.

D. **Danger from Scotland.**

    Hostility of the Regent Albany, who was inclined to form an alliance with France.

E. **Danger from France.**

    Charles VI was apparently willing to take up the cause of Richard II, his son-in-law. Difficulties arose as to the position of Richard's widow, Queen Isabella.

F. **Great danger from Wales.**

    Owen Glendower, a Welsh gentleman, learned, refined, a soldier trained in the suite of Arundel, and a landowner, quarrelled with Lord Grey of Ruthin. Henry confiscated or alienated his estates, and made him a rebel. This personal quarrel became later a national rising.

BARONIAL REBELLIONS
AGAINST HENRY IV

I. General.

A. Note the cleavage in the barons, which, beginning with the execution of Gaveston, continued in the reigns of Richard II and Henry IV, and culminated in the Wars of the Roses.

B. Rebellion had been easy in the reign of Richard II, and the barons in Henry IV's reign were consequently inclined to revolt.

C. Richard, alive, formed a centre of revolt, and after he was killed many believed him to be still alive.

D. Henry's successful rising against Richard had sanctioned the idea that "default of governance" justified deposition, and this idea justified rebellion when his own government failed.

E. Henry put down all the rebellions of the barons, but did not break the power of the barons, to which the fall of the House of Lancaster was finally due.

II. Actual Rebellions.

A. The Earls of Huntingdon and Kent (half-brother and nephew of Richard, who had lost the titles of Dukes of Surrey and Exeter), the Earl of Salisbury and Lord Despenser plotted to kill Henry at Windsor and proclaim Richard. The plot was revealed by a traitor (probably Rutland, son of the Duke of York). Kent and Salisbury were executed by the people at Cirencester; Huntingdon and Despenser slain by mobs in Essex and at Bristol, **1400.**

Result: The death of Richard at Pontefract.

(1) He was said to have starved himself to death.

(2) He probably died owing to rigorous ill-treatment.

(3) He was not slain by Exton as Shakespeare suggests.

(4) The corpse was exposed to view in London, but many believed that Richard was still alive in Scotland.

B. The Percies.

The Earl of Northumberland, the constable, the Earl of Worcester, his brother, the admiral, and Northumberland's son, Harry Hotspur, warden of the North Welsh Marches.

(1) **1399.** Northumberland had ensured the succession of Henry IV, and had lent him money which had not been repaid.

(2) **1402.** At Homildon Hill, in Northumberland, the Percies had captured Douglas and Murdoch, the nephew of the King of Scotland. The King demanded their ransoms, which the Percies claimed for themselves.

(3) Henry did not give Hotspur sufficient forces to check Glendower, who now styled himself " Prince of Wales " and raised the national standard of the dragon.

(4) The King refused to ransom Hotspur's brother-in-law, Mortimer, who had been captured by Glendower.

    1403. *a.* A league was formed against Henry between Glendower, the Percies, Douglas (released by the Percies), and Mortimer, who had married Glendower's daughter and supported the claim of his nephew, Edmund Earl of March, to the throne.

        1. Glendower failed to join forces with Hotspur, who was defeated and slain at Shrewsbury, where Worcester was captured and executed.

        2. Northumberland, who had remained in the north, was pardoned by the King.

        3. Successes of Glendower, aided by the French, in South Wales and capture of Cardiff. The French sacked Plymouth and attacked the Isle of Wight.

    1405. *β.* Second rising of Northumberland, supported by Mowbray (son of the Duke of Norfolk) and Scrope Archbishop of York, who joined as a protest against the bad government of Henry IV. Scrope and Mowbray were captured by trickery by the Earl of Westmorland and executed. Great outcry at the execution of Scrope, and the skin disease (which was not leprosy) from which Henry suffered henceforth was regarded as a divine punishment for the deed.

Escape of Northumberland to Scotland, and many executions in Yorkshire and Northumberland.

γ. Third rising of Northumberland, who was defeated and slain at Bramham Moor, near Tadcaster, **1408**.

(5) Danger at home ceased after this victory.

α. The Percies were crushed.

β. The Prince of Wales captured Aberystwith and Harlech, and broke the power of Glendower, who was often obliged to lie "hid in caves and thickets" to escape his enemies.

γ. The capture of Prince James of Scotland, **1405**, gave Henry a means of preventing attacks from Scotland, as the Regent Albany gladly made peace with Henry to ensure the imprisonment of his nephew James and his own consequent supremacy in Scotland.

δ. But domestic politics were complicated by a quarrel between Archbishop Arundel and the Prince of Wales, supported by the Beauforts, sons of John of Gaunt and Katharine Swynford (Henry Bishop of Lincoln and Winchester, and afterwards Cardinal, and his brother John Earl of Somerset).

ε. France was weakened by the quarrel between the Orleanists or Armagnacs[1] (supporting Louis of Orleans, younger brother of King Charles VI, who had become insane) and the Burgundians (supporting Philip the Bold, the youngest son of King John, and uncle of King Charles VI and Louis of Orleans). The quarrel due to the attempts of Louis and Philip to secure the regency of France.

---

[1] The name Armagnac was derived from Bernard of Armagnac (the father-in-law of Louis' son Charles), who became the leader of the Orleanists after the murder of Louis.

1407. The quarrel became a civil war, when Louis was assassinated in Paris by order of John the Fearless, who had succeeded his father Philip as Duke of Burgundy.

This civil war saved England from the danger of French invasion.

References :

A. *The Political History of England, 1377–1485*, by Oman, Longmans, chap. VII. and pp. 187–204.

Owen Glendower, *Heroes of the Nations*, pp. 302–9.

B. Shakespeare, *Henry IV*, Part I :—

HOMILDON HILL (ACT I, *Scene* 3): "My liege, I did deny no prisoners."

GLENDOWER (ACT. III, *Scene* 1): "In faith, he is a worthy gentleman."

HOTSPUR (ACT III, *Scene* 2): "And even as I was then is Percy now."

Chevy Chase.

C. *Fair Maid of Perth*, Scott.

Both Sides of the Border, by Henley, Blackie.

Cambria's Chieftain, by Everett Green, Nelson.

The Caged Lion, by Yonge, Macmillan.

PARLIAMENT AND HENRY IV

I. **The King was dependent upon Parliament,** which had elected him, on the support of which the continuation of his house depended, and from which alone he could get the grants necessary to carry on the government.

Henry IV was very poor; he possessed the hereditary estates of Lancaster, but received no revenue from Wales, and had to meet heavy expenses owing to

α. The Welsh, Scotch, and French wars and the baronial rebellions.

β. The cost of the fleet and of the defence of Calais.

γ. The cost of the royal household.

He was so poor that he had to borrow £6000 from Richard Whittington, thrice Mayor (*not* Lord Mayor) of London, whose successful trading in a vessel called the *Cat* led to the famous popular story.

Therefore began the "Lancastrian experiment," government by limited monarchy. This failed because it was premature, as the Commons were not equal to the task till the seventeenth century. But the power of Henry IV was greatly limited, although towards the end of his reign this tactful "practical, wary personage" regained some of the power which he had lost, and the concessions he made gained for his house the strong support of the Commons.

II. The Work of Henry's Parliaments.

A. Settlement.

(1) Confirmation of the proceedings of the Merciless Parliament, **1388**, and reversal of those of the Shrewsbury Parliament, **1398**. This caused great disputes as to the legal ownership of land, and led to repeated challenges to battle even in Parliament.

(2) Appeals of treason were finally forbidden.

(3) Trial of Richard II's supporters; mild measures, little bloodshed; some titles were revoked, e.g. the Dukes of Surrey and Exeter were degraded to the position of Earls of Kent and Huntingdon (page 195).

B. Parliament and the Church.

(1) **1401.** Passed the Statute de Heretico Comburendo, an acknowledgment of Henry's orthodoxy and of his gratitude to Arundel. Heretics refusing to abjure to be handed over to secular authorities and publicly burned. The statute was generally accepted, as the Church was fairly popular, in spite of its great wealth and the Great Schism, and the principle that heretics deserved death was generally accepted; but Lollardy was not extinguished, and in the Parliament of **1410** there was "an execrable crowd of Lollard knights."

(2) **1404.** The Unlearned Parliament (so called because lawyers were excluded) suggested the confiscation of one year's income of all ecclesiastical property.

(3) **1410.** The Commons pointed out that the estates of the Church would endow fifteen earls, 1500 knights, 6200 esquires, and 100 hospitals.

C. Parliament and the King.

(1) **1401.** The right of freedom of speech in Parliament was recognised by the King.

(2) Complaints of bad governance.

1404. Complaints of expenses and failure of the Welsh expedition.

1406. Demand of good governance and presentation of thirty-one articles of reform, which were accepted by Henry, although they seriously limited the executive power of the Crown.

(3) Finance.

The Commons wished the King "to live of his own," i.e. to meet all his expenses out of the ordinary revenue derived from customs, ferms of the counties, feudal dues, and forests. This was quite impossible, and the ordinary revenue was supplemented by Parliamentary grants. Therefore the Commons tried to get control of the grants they were compelled to make.

1401. Parliament resolved that the King should not make grants without the consent of the Council. This resolution was due to lavish grants made to the Percies and others. The King refused to accept it.

1401. A petition of the Commons that redress of grievances should precede supply was evaded by the King.

1404. Treasurers were appointed to administer grants made to meet the cost of the Welsh and Scottish wars.

1406. Auditors were appointed to audit the account of the grants of **1404**.

1407. Money grants to originate in the Commons and to be declared by the Speaker.

(4) Considerable interference with the King's household.

1404. Queen Joan compelled to send away many of her Breton followers.

1406. Protest against the "rascalry" composing the King's household.

(5) The settlement of the Succession.

1406. The Crown was guaranteed to Henry's heirs.

(6) The influence of the sheriffs over Parliamentary elections was limited by Parliament on three occasions, in **1406**, **1410**, and **1413**.

(7) The Royal Council.

    α. Gradual growth of the importance of the Privy Council from the reign of Henry III. In the time of Richard II it had become a power co-ordinate with the King, and it exercised great authority in the reign of Henry IV owing to the bad health, weak claim and poverty of the King.

    β. The Council dealt with finance, trade, Church questions, the interpretation of treaties, and the maintenance of order, and acted as a court of appeal.

    γ. Parliament was anxious to curtail the authority of the Royal Council, which was prejudicial to its own, and under Henry IV succeeded in securing control of the nomination of its members, **1404**, **1406**, and **1410**.

1406. Appointment in Parliament of a " Continual Council " of seventeen to hold office until next Parliament, to choose sheriffs, and to give grants.

1412. The " Continual Council " abolished. The abolition was a proof of the growing power of the King.

Reference :

A. Stubbs' *Constitutional History*, Vol. III, pp. 1–73.

THE HUNDRED YEARS' WAR AND THE LANCASTRIANS

I. Henry IV.

Less danger from France owing to the division between the Orleanists and Burgundians. See page **197**. England made an alliance with both as seemed convenient, and English diplomacy proved adroit and unscrupulous.

1407. The assassination of Louis of Orleans by agents of Burgundy aggravated the division.

1411. English alliance with Burgundy supported by the Prince of Wales. England helped Burgundy to defend Paris (which favoured Burgundy) and to defeat the Orleanist besiegers at St. Cloud.

1412. Disgraceful alliance made by Arundel, in spite of the opposition of the Prince of Wales, with the Orleanists, who offered to restore Aquitaine to Henry IV. Failure of Clarence's expedition to support the Orleanists.

But under Henry IV,

1. No claim was made to the French crown.
2. There was no settled policy in regard to France.

II. **Henry V.**

A. The renewal of the war.

(1) Henry's claim to the French crown marks a change in policy.

α. He claimed the Angevin Empire of Henry II, and also Ponthieu, Provence, and Boulogne.

β. He revived the claims of Edward III to the French crown, although the denial of the Salic Law, which made this claim possible, would have justified the claim of Edmund Earl of March to the crown of England.

(2) The state of France.

α. Continued dissensions between the Burgundians and Armagnacs.

β. Charles VI was mad. (Cards were invented to amuse him.)

γ. Queen Isabella of Bavaria was vicious and at enmity with Charles the Dauphin (afterwards Charles VII).

δ. The feeling of nationality in France was dormant.

(3) Henry's claim was supported by

α. The clergy, because a foreign war would distract attention from clerical abuses and divert attacks (largely Lollard) upon their wealth.

(**1414.** Confiscation of alien priories.)

Hence the hearty support of Henry Beaufort, Bishop of Winchester.

β. The nobles were ready for a war which would
bring fame and plunder. Henry IV had
checked but had not broken the power of the
nobles. The French war for a time ended
baronial quarrels in England. No conspiracies,
except that of Richard of Cambridge, were
made in Henry V's reign.

γ. The merchants, because of the damage done to
English shipping by Norman privateers.

(4) The war was unprovoked, unjustifiable, but popular. It
caused endless suffering in France, but out of successful resistance came the growth of nationality. In
England it was one of the causes of the Wars of the
Roses and the overthrow of the Lancastrian House.

The French offered most liberal terms—two-thirds
of Aquitaine, a dowry of 800,000 crowns, with the
hand of Princess Katharine. Refused by Henry V.

B. The Agincourt Campaign.

(1) **1415.** The capture of Harfleur gave a base of operations with easy communication with England.

(2) The March towards Calais.

Foolish and reckless. Henry's army was small, "weak
with want of victuals" and dysentery (due partly to
eating raw chestnuts).

(3) The Battle of Agincourt.

a. The French (at least five times as many as the
English)

1. Took up a position in a defile between
two woods, which prevented them from
using their superior numbers to outflank
the English.

2. Drew up their army in three divisions;
hopeless confusion arose when the first
two were defeated.

    3. Relied on heavy-armed men, the weight of whose armour prevented speedy attack on the muddy ground and rendered flight impossible. Hence an enormous number, greater than the total of Henry's army, were slain.

    4. No use was made of a large force of French archers.

β. The English.

    1. Their line was equal in length, but not in depth, to the French line.

    2. The English archers, protected by stakes, drove back the French heavy cavalry, whose wounded horses threw the rear into confusion.

    3. The English attacked the second line— heavy-armed infantry—who were easily routed through the weight of their armour and very close order.

    4. The French prisoners were killed by Henry's orders owing to a false alarm that another French force had fallen upon the rear.

γ. Criticism.

    1. A great feat of arms. The English had no advantage of higher position as at Creçy and Poitiers. The archers again rendered most valuable service.

    2. This victory gave England a position in Europe, led to an alliance with the Emperor Sigismund, discouraged the French, but led to little permanent gain, except the ransom of prisoners and a safe retreat.

    3. Further success was due to dissensions in France, not to the victory at Agincourt.

C. The Conquest of Normandy.

A campaign of conquest most skilfully executed. Pillage and arson were rigorously put down. An attack on Paris by Burgundy and a quarrel between Queen Isabella and the Armagnac regent prevented effective help from being sent to Normandy.

1417. Conquest of the central coast line, Caen, Bayeux, Lisieux, by Henry.

1419. John the Fearless, Duke of Burgundy, after capturing Paris and massacring his Armagnac opponents, concluded an alliance with the Dauphin, but was foully murdered by Tanneguy du Châtel while paying homage to the Dauphin on the bridge of Montereau. His son, Philip the Good, therefore embraced the English cause.

Fall of Rouen. Ready submission of the Rouennais, who distrusted both Burgundy and the Dauphin, to Henry.

An attempt was made to set up "another England in Normandy." Introduction of the English military and judicial organisation, and of English settlers.

D. The Treaty of Troyes **1420.**

The Conquest of Normandy and the alliance of England with Burgundy led to the Treaty of Troyes.

(1) Henry was to be regent during the lifetime of Charles VI and to succeed him.

(2) Henry was to marry Katharine without a dowry.

(3) The Dauphin Charles was expressly excluded from the throne.

    a. A personal, not a corporate, union of England and France. The French were to keep their own laws and liberties.

    β. The growth of the feeling of nationality in France and England was sure to make permanent union impossible.

1421. Defeat and death of Clarence at Beaugé by the French and Scotch under the Earl of Buchan.

1422. Henry captured Dreux and Meaux.

August 31, 1422. Henry died of dysentery.

III. **Bedford's Rule, 1422-1435.**

  A. Bedford's position.

    (1) Bedford was an excellent regent. He governed France by Frenchmen sitting in "estates." Very few English officials, and no English bishops, were appointed.

    (2) He married Anne, the sister of Philip the Good, and thus strengthened the Burgundian alliance. He made an alliance with Brittany, thus protecting the borders of the English possessions, the shape of which was a triangle with its apex at Paris.

    (3) The difficulties of his position.

        α. The English had not enough men to garrison the country.

        β. Humphrey Duke of Gloucester (Bedford's younger brother)

            1. 1423. Married Jacqueline of Hainault without the consent of her feudal superior, Burgundy, who hoped ultimately to secure her possessions.

                Consequent alienation of Burgundy. English soldiers required for service in France were used to conquer Hainault.

            2. 1425. Bedford was compelled to return home to settle a quarrel between Gloucester and Henry Beaufort, who was acting as Regent of England. His absence weakened the English cause in France.

  B. Joan of Arc.

    (1) Charles, in the hands of wicked advisers, had "lost nerve" owing to the murder of John the Fearless; he was dissolute, weak, and harassed by doubts as to the legitimacy of his birth, caused by the immorality of his mother, Isabel of Bavaria.

    (2) The English had won the battles of Crevant, 1423, and Verneuil, 1424, and in 1428 attacked Orleans, the strongest town of the French frontier. It was bravely defended by Dunois, but his friends sent no help, and Sir John Fastolf, by making a square of his

1429. wagons, won the "Battle of Herrings" at Rouvrai. Surrender seemed inevitable.

(3) Joan of Arc appeared. A career unique in history.

    a. She was an illiterate peasant girl, who believed that she had been inspired by the "voices" of St. Michael and other angels.

    β. Unaided she singled out Charles from his courtiers and won his support by giving him divine assurance of his legitimacy.

    γ. Four bishops reported most favourably on her character and orthodoxy.

    δ. She got safely into Orleans, inspired the garrison, who called her the "Maid of God," raised the siege and defeated the English at Jargeau

1429. and Patay. Charles was crowned at Rheims.

1430. Joan failed to take Paris, was captured at Compiègne, and in May, **1431,** burnt as a witch at Rouen. Her execution was due to the cruelty of Bedford, to the obsequiousness of his French supporters, especially Pierre Cauchon, Bishop of Beauvais, and to the gross and criminal ingratitude of Charles VII, who did not try to save her, owing to the representations of his servants, who were jealous of her influence

    1. She had recaptured the Loire valley, much of Champagne and of the Isle of France.

    2. She had roused the national spirit in spite of the apathy of the followers of Charles VII, and this was seen in Normandy later.

C. Bedford's difficulties.

(1) Gloucester was causing further difficulty in England, where enthusiasm for the war had cooled, and a peace party had arisen under Henry Beaufort, Bishop of Winchester.

(2) Burgundy (whose alliance had been maintained only by the cession of land in the north-west and north-east of France) made a treaty with Charles.

(3) Death of Anne, the wife of Bedford and sister of Philip the Good, **1432.**

(4) Marriage of Bedford to Jacquetta of Luxemburg, daughter of Burgundy's vassal, the Count of St. Pol. Burgundy was angry either because he was not consulted or because of the speedy remarriage of his brother-in-law.

(5) Rising of the peasantry in Normandy—very serious. It showed the growth of anti-English sentiment in a hitherto obedient province.

(6) Paris was famine-stricken. (Wolves were seen in the suburbs in 1434.) Great dissatisfaction with the English rule.

D. The Congress of Arras, 1435.

Owing to the strong representations of Burgundy a conference was held at Arras between the English and French.

The French offered to give up Normandy and Guienne, for which the English were to pay homage, if the English withdrew all claims to the French throne and to any other part of France, including Calais. The English refused all terms because the French insisted that the title of King of France should be given up. The refusal of the liberal offer of the French for the sake of an empty title was utter folly, especially as the English had steadily lost ground recently in spite of the support of Burgundy.

Death of Bedford, 15 September, 1435. Burgundy finally gave up the English cause, which never recovered from the loss of the Burgundian alliance.

IV. The loss of France, 1435–53.

A. A gallant effort was made by the English governor of Normandy, Richard Duke of York.

1437. York captured Pontoise commanding the Seine valley.

Edmund Beaufort took Harfleur.

B. The Peace party in England was growing stronger, and included Suffolk and the Beauforts (especially Edmund Beaufort, who succeeded his brother John as Earl of Somerset).

   1445. Suffolk arranged the marriage of Henry VI to Margaret of Anjou, hoping thus to end the war and to ensure the possession of Normandy and Guienne. But he only secured a truce and promised to surrender Anjou and Maine. Maine was actually surrendered **1448.**

   Queen Margaret and Henry VI strongly supported Suffolk and peace. Gloucester, "the Good Duke Humphrey," the leader of the war party, lost influence on the condemnation of his wife Eleanor Cobham for witchcraft, and was arrested and died (probably murdered) at Calais. Suffolk, whose friends got much of his lands, was accused of the murder. It was a foolish deed, as Richard of York was far more able than Gloucester, and now became heir-presumptive.

C. **1449.** The loss of Normandy.

   The English broke the truce. Four French armies under Dunois and Charles VII invaded Eastern Normandy, which fell easily because it was badly garrisoned and because the people had turned against the English. The people of Rouen opened their gates, **1449.** The English were routed at Formigny **1450**, and York's successor, Somerset, an incompetent governor, was compelled to surrender. The rest of Normandy lost.

D. The loss of Guienne.

   Dunois captured Bordeaux and Bayonne, but the French were unpopular owing to their exactions and the Gascons urged the English to attempt to regain the towns.

   1452. Bordeaux revolted.

   1453. Talbot, Earl of Shrewsbury, was sent to help Bordeaux and reconquer Guienne, but was routed and slain at Châtillon.

   Submission of Guienne, although its strong English

P

sympathies were shown by the resolute defence of some smaller towns.

Calais alone was left in English hands.

References :

A. Lodge, *Close of the Middle Ages*, Rivingtons, pp. 320-58.

B. Shakespeare, *Henry V :—*

> ACT III, *Scene* 1 : "Once more unto the breach, dear friends, once more."
>
> ACT IV, *Scene* 3 : "What's he that wishes so?"

Drayton's *Battle of Agincourt*.
Green's *Short History of the English People*, pp. 274-9.

C. *At Agincourt*, by Henty. Blackie.
A Monk of Fife, by Lang. Longmans.
Noemi, by Baring Gould. Methuen.

CHARACTER OF HENRY V

I. His Youth.

The popular view that in his earlier life he was utterly dissolute is wrong. He did not drink habitually in Eastcheap taverns with lowborn associates, and did not strike Gascoigne, and the dismissal of Gascoigne on Henry's accession was not an act of mean revenge, but due to the age of Gascoigne.

He undertook heavy responsibility as Prince of Wales, showed great military skill in his campaigns against Glendower (capturing Aberystwith in **1408** and Harlech in **1409**) and took an active part in the work of the Council, where, in conjunction with the Beauforts, he strongly advocated the policy of alliance with the Burgundians. But he was guilty of occasional lapses into vice. On his accession to the throne "sodaynly he became a new man."

II. **As King.**

    A. His policy.

        (1) The French war, from a modern point of view,
unjustifiable. But Henry was probably convinced of
his right to the crown and felt that he ought to
follow the hereditary tradition of English kings,
viz. war with France. He was strongly supported by
the whole nation. He felt justified in this policy
owing to his determination to use the power gained
by the expected conquest of France in a campaign
against the Turks for the deliverance of Jerusalem.

            The French war made him "the greatest king in
Christendom" and England the leading country in
Europe. This is shown by the visit of Sigismund in
1416, and by the fact that the Great Schism was ended
at the Council of Constance owing partly to Henry's
influence.

1416. A great league was formed by the skilful diplomacy
of Henry between England, Holland, Bavaria, the
Hanse Towns, and Burgundy.

            But his foreign policy, though successful for a time
owing to his personal popularity and military success,
was entirely wrong. The growing feeling of nationality
in England and France rendered the union of the two
countries impossible. His death showed the folly of his
policy, which in France caused endless misery ending
in national union, and in England led to the Wars of
the Roses and the fall of the House of Lancaster.

        (2) At home he was a "reconciling and uniting force." His
military policy won the support of the clergy, nobles,
and people, and Richard of Cambridge's was the only
baronial rising in his reign.

            He won over possible opponents by moderation.

            α. John Holland, son of the Earl of Huntingdon,
who had rebelled against Henry IV (p. 195),
and the son of Hotspur, were restored to lands
and honours as the Earls of Huntingdon and
Northumberland.

β. Edmund Earl of March was received into high favour, in spite of his hereditary claim to the throne and of Cambridge's rebellion on his behalf.

γ. Richard of York, son of Cambridge, was brought up at court.

But the execution of Cambridge, though justified by his rebellion, continued the "tradition of bloodshed," and his descendants overthrew Henry VI.

B. As a soldier.

(1) He was a great general in the field.

(2) The campaign of 1417–1419 was skilfully conducted.

(3) His careful attention to details helped to win the affection of his soldiers.

(4) He was generally merciful to conquered enemies (e.g. the people of Rouen).

a. The execution of Alan Blanchard (the captain of the crossbowmen at Rouen) was justified by his previous conduct.

β. The slaughter of French prisoners at Agincourt was apparently justified by the necessities of the case, but the execution of the Scotch prisoners taken at Meaux, and of a trumpeter simply for blowing a defiant blast against the King at Meaux, cannot be justified.

(5) The march from Harfleur, 1415, was reckless and foolhardy and the victory at Agincourt does not justify it.

C. His religion.

He was sincerely and devoutly pious.

(1) He wished to prove by a crusade that he was "the most Christian Champion of the Church."

(2) He persecuted the Lollards.

a. The persecution of heretics was regarded as a duty by mediæval kings.

β. Henry V was not fond of persecution. He tried to convert the Lollard Badby at the stake, and thus to save his life.

γ. The Lollards were politically dangerous owing to their connection with Wales, where Cobham found refuge.

D. He restored the navy.

Built ships. His naval ordinances, rather than those of Richard I, are the foundation of our Admiralty law.

He appointed naval surgeons and took measures for victualling the ships.

E. His character.

(1) He was probably sincere, though apt to take a narrow view when his own interests were concerned.

(2) He felt the grave responsibility of his position and showed this in his dignified and solemn manners.

(3) Shakespeare's Henry V is a more accurate picture than Prince Hal.

(4) He was a "typical mediæval hero" and "the flower and glory of knighthood." In spite of faults of action and policy he stands for patriotism and the glory of England, and thus resembles Queen Elizabeth.

References :

A. *English Men of Action*, "Henry V," pp. 152–5.

B. Shakespeare, *Henry V :—*

ACT IV, *Scene* 1 : "Upon the King ! let us our lives, our souls."

C. *Every Inch a King*, by Sawyer, Dodd, Mead, and Co., and *Agincourt*, by James, Warne.

JACK CADE'S REBELLION, 1450

I. Gross Misgovernment of the Kingdom.

Suffolk was unable to gain success abroad or to ensure peace at home. At home the "Lancastrian experiment" failed because the barons were "overmighty," the Church, largely political, had lost influence, and the King was utterly incapable. There was no one able and willing to redress the abuses of the time.

II. Cade.

There is little definite information about Jack Cade, he was possibly Irish; he called himself Mortimer; he had served under York in France, and was a man of education and military skill. He was possibly in secret league with the enemies of Suffolk; he supported the Duke of York, who, in 1459, was accused of complicity in the rebellion.

III. The Rising.

A. Causes.

General dissatisfaction with the ministry, especially with the conduct of the French war. The immediate cause was the defeat of the English at Formigny in 1450, followed by the impeachment, flight, and murder at sea of Suffolk. His body was washed up on the coast of Kent, which was threatened with devastation by the King in consequence.

B. The rising of Kent under Cade "to correct public abuses and to remove evil counsellors." The "Complaint of the Commons of Kent" protested against

α. The loss of France,

β. The murder of Humphrey of Gloucester,

γ. Financial mismanagement—

(1) The waste of public money,

(2) The failure to pay the King's debts,

(3) The heavy taxes,

(4) The extortion of officials,

δ. The interference of barons and sheriffs in Parliamentary elections;

and demanded

α. The banishment of the supporters of Suffolk,

β. The admission of York to the Council,

γ. The abolition of the Statute of Labourers.

The rebel army of 20,000 men at Blackheath was well armed and well organised. It defeated at Sevenoaks a royal army disaffected through lack of pay. Cade entered London without opposition, and murdered Lord Saye, the Treasurer. The Londoners, roused to resistance by the pillage of their houses, defended London Bridge against Cade. The rebels dispersed on a promise of pardon. Cade's was revoked because it was granted in the name of "John Mortimer," and he was slain by the Sheriff of Kent. A second rising in Kent utterly failed.

Risings in Norfolk and Wiltshire (where Ayscough Bishop of Salisbury was slain) were easily suppressed.

IV. Importance of the Rising.

A. It was a proof of the general discontent with the incapable Lancastrian government.

B. It was mainly political—although the rebels demanded the abolition of the Statute of Labourers—and was thus different from the Peasants' Revolt.

C. It revealed the utter weakness of the King, who was quite unable to control the barons.

D. It is quite possible that Cade received secret encouragement from the Yorkists, but there is no definite proof of this.

References:

A. Stubbs' *Constitutional History*, Vol. III, pp. 155–7.

B. *King Henry VI*, Part II:—

Act IV, *Scene* 2: "We Jack Cade, so termed of our supposed father,"

CAUSES OF THE WARS
OF THE ROSES

The Weakness of the Lancastrian Rule.

A. The failure of its foreign policy.

The loss of Normandy (inevitable, but popular anger was aggravated by the mismanagement and incompetence of Somerset, Governor **1448–1450**) and Guienne.

Anger at the surrender of Maine **1448**, a condition of the marriage of Henry and Margaret which took place **1445**.

B. Its failure at home was shown by Jack Cade's rebellion.
"The realm of England was out of all good governance."

(1) The "Lancastrian experiment" of limited monarchy had broken down. The Commons had secured great constitutional power, but "constitutional progress had outrun administrative order," and the country was not yet ready for self-government.

(2) The King was poor, the finances badly managed, money and grants were recklessly bestowed on favourites and friends of the Queen.

(3) The King was too weak to control the barons, to put down the "sturdy beggars" who increased in numbers owing to the smaller demand for agricultural labourers through the introduction of sheep-farming and to the discharge of soldiers and sailors at the close of the French war.

(4) The law was badly administered—there was little protection for the weak against the strong.

II. **The Excessive Power of the Great Barons—the "Overmighty Subject."**

A. Two great factions—"a dynastic cleavage of the barons."

1. The Yorkist, whose centre was the Nevilles.

The head, Richard of York (son of Richard Earl of Cambridge and Anne Mortimer), united the Mortimer and York estates and married Cicely, daughter of Ralph Earl of Westmorland.

Richard Neville I, the younger son of Ralph, married Alice Montacute, the heiress of the Earl of Salisbury killed at Orleans 1429. His brothers were Barons Latimer, Fauconberg, and Abergavenny.

Richard Neville II, son of the above, married Anne Beauchamp, heiress of the Earl of Warwick.

John Mowbray, Duke of Norfolk, son of Richard Neville's sister.

Lord Bourchier married York's sister Isabella.

Thomas Bourchier was made Archbishop of Canterbury.

THE NEVILLES

RALPH NEVILLE, EARL OF WESTMORLAND

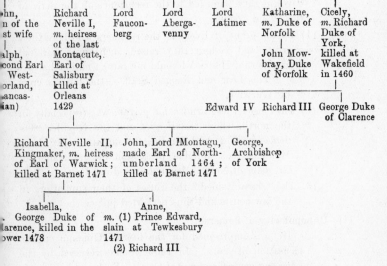

RICHARD EARL OF CAMBRIDGE
m. Anne Mortimer

Richard Duke of York

Isabella, *m.* Lord Bourchier

(2) The Lancastrian party included the majority of the House of Lords, especially Edmund Duke of Somerset (created Duke **1448** and killed at St. Albans **1455**) and the Beaufort connection,

Percy Earl of Northumberland,

The Duke of Buckingham,

Ralph Earl of Westmorland, the head of the elder branch of the Nevilles (i.e. the children of Ralph, first Earl of Westmorland, by his first wife, who were jealous of the power of Richard Neville and the other children of the second wife).

The Queen was a strong supporter of this party, and by her conduct made the King the nominal head of a faction and gravely weakened his position.

B. Their vast estates and enormous wealth made the barons "overmighty," and led to the recurrence of the evils of the feudal system.

(1) By the grant of livery to the retainers who bore their crests and badges they raised such great baronial armies that Henry VI could not raise a national army.

"The Bear and Ragged Staff"—the famous crest of Warwick.

(2) They used these armies for private war (especially in the north, where the Percies and the Nevilles were fierce enemies) and for illegal usurpations (e.g. Lord Moleyns took forcible possession of the manor of Gresham in Norfolk belonging to John Paston).

(3) They "maintained" the causes of their supporters in the law courts and thus perverted justice.

III. **Unpopularity of Somerset.**

He was imprisoned for the loss of Guienne on the accusation of York. In **1455** he was released by the King and made Governor of Calais. York and his friends were not summoned to the Council, and took up arms in self-defence against Somerset, who was slain at the "ill day of St. Albans." Thus the first battle of the Wars of the Roses was due to constitutional causes, viz.

(1) An outbreak against an unpopular minister,

(2) The assertion of the right of York to attend the Council.
The death of Somerset made the Queen the head of the Lancastrians.

IV. **Queen Margaret was most unpopular.**

She was "the strength and weakness of the royal cause."

A. Her marriage was associated with the loss of Maine and Anjou.

B. She was a strong supporter of the party of Suffolk and Somerset.

C. She tried to stir up the French to attack Warwick when he was Governor of Calais, the "wild Irish" against York when Lord Lieutenant of Ireland 1449–50, and the Scotch against the northern Yorkists. She also gave Berwick to the Scotch.

D. She gave her badge (the Swan) to the men of Cheshire in 1459, and this was one of the causes of York's second rising.

E. Her vindictive policy at Coventry 1459 (when York and his friends were attainted), and her cruelty after her victories at Wakefield 1460 and second St. Albans 1461, aggravated the struggle.

F. She refused to recognise York as heir after the battle of Northampton 1460, and took up arms to assert the right of her son. Thus the war, commenced to overthrow an unpopular minister, became a struggle for the crown.

V. **The Claim to the Throne.**

A. The Lancastrians' claim, resting on the grant of Parliament and prescription, was valid, in spite of their "defect of genealogy." They were the "heirs male." Henry VI said: "My father was king; his father was also king; I myself have worn the crown forty years from my cradle."

B. The Yorkists were "heirs general" claiming in female line through Lionel of Clarence (elder brother of John of Gaunt), and in male line through Edmund of Langley, Duke of York (younger brother of John of Gaunt). But

   (1) York had taken the oath of allegiance to the Lancastrians, and

   (2) He had used the arms of Langley and not Clarence, and this weakened his claim.

C. Any possible claim through the Beauforts was barred by the statute of **1407**, which expressly denied their right to succeed. But Henry VII based his claim partly (incorrectly) on his descent from John of Gaunt through his mother, Margaret Beaufort.

D. York apparently did not claim the throne until **1460**, when Margaret's persistent attacks led to the claim. His claim to supersede Henry VI at once was strongly opposed by Warwick and refused by Parliament.

E. Edward IV's accession was a "legitimist restoration," warranted by the urgent need of strong and good government and not by his hereditary claims.

VI. **The tone of the Nation had been lowered by the unjust war with France.** The century was one of low ideals and of selfish materialism. Striking poverty of literature. The influence of the Church was very weak, and there was great immorality among the nobles. The Wars of the Roses displayed a lack of chivalry, religion, and morality.

References :

A. *Political History of England, 1377–1485*, by Oman, pp. 352–62.

B. Shakespeare, *Henry VI :—*

   PART II, ACT I, *Scene* 1 : "Anjou and Maine are given to the French."

   PART III, ACT I, *Scene* 1 : "Enforced thee ! art thou King and wilt be forced ?"

THE WARS OF THE ROSES

I. **Geographical Division of Parties.**

A. **The North.**

(1) The Yorkists were strong in the north, although the power of the Nevilles in Durham and the North Riding was balanced by

   a. The Percies,

   β. Ralph, second Earl of Westmorland, head of the elder branch of the Nevilles.

(2) After Northampton, **1460**, Margaret roused the Northerners and won the battle of Wakefield, **1460**, with their help.

(3) The Yorkist victory at Towton, **1461**, gave Edward IV command of the country up to the Tees.

(4) Northumberland, though conquered by Warwick, rose in favour of the Lancastrians in **1464**, when Sir Ralph Grey and the Duke of Somerset broke their oaths of allegiance to Edward. The victories of Montagu at Hedgeley Moor and Hexham, and the capture of Bamborough Castle, completed the Yorkist conquest of England.

B. **The Midlands.**

In the west the Mortimer interest ensured the Yorkist supremacy on the Welsh Marches.

The cruelties following Wakefield **1460**, the execution of Salisbury, the murder of Rutland, the mutilation of York's body—his head was stuck on Micklegate Bar at York crowned with a paper crown—and the excesses of Margaret's Northern army who stole the sacred vessels from churches, alienated the Midlands from the Lancastrian cause.

C. London.

    (1) Yorkist, especially after the excesses of the Lancastrians after second St. Albans, **1461**.

    (2) The great importance of London was shown, 1461, by the race for London between Edward Earl of March (who had defeated Jasper Tudor at Mortimer's Cross) and Margaret (who had won the battle of Wakefield).

    (3) Margaret's failure to push on to London, which had been abandoned by the Yorkist leaders after second St. Albans, was apparently a grave blunder.

D. The South.

    The towns of the south tended to support the Yorkists in the hope that they would ensure the "good governance" necessary for trade.

    Somerset supported the Lancastrian cause in the south-west.

E. East Anglia.

    Yorkist owing to the influence of John Mowbray, Duke of Norfolk, nephew of Salisbury.

F. Kent.

    Yorkist owing to the influence of Warwick, who found in Calais, of which he was Warden, a safe refuge, as Richard of York did in Ireland.

G. Wales.

    Lancastrian owing to the influence of the Tudors, sons of Katherine of France (widow of Henry V) and Owen Tudor. Their power was broken by the defeat by Edward at Mortimer's Cross of Jasper Tudor, Earl of Pembroke (uncle of Henry of Richmond, afterwards Henry VII).

II. Periods of the War.

A. First Period, **1455–1459**.

    (1) Opposition to an unpopular minister (Somerset) and the claim of the Yorkist leaders to attend the Council, i.e. constitutional questions, were the immediate cause of the war.

(2) The war was not at first vindictive. At first St. Albans only "some six score slain"—possibly fewer.

(3) The Yorkists lost ground. They won the battle of Bloreheath, but their leaders, attainted at Coventry, fled from England after Ludlow, 1459, and might have been crushed but for the failure of the Lancastrians to make the most of their opportunities.

B. Second Period, 1459-1461.

(1) Change in the nature of the struggle, which became dynastic owing to York's fear of Margaret's power (which led him to claim the crown to strengthen his position) and Margaret's attempt to gain the crown for her son in spite of the recognition of York as heir after Northampton 1460.

(2) Great success of the Yorkists—Mortimer's Cross 1460, Towton 1461. But the Yorkist cause was weakened by the deaths of York and Salisbury at Wakefield 1460, and Margaret's victory at second St. Albans 1461.

(3) Growing cruelty to prisoners. The war became a baronial blood feud.

a. At Northampton, 1460, Warwick gave orders to spare the commons, but at Towton, 1461, the leaders on both sides ordered no quarter to be given, and 35,000 men were slain.

β. Gross cruelty shown by Margaret after Wakefield and second St. Albans, when she made Prince Edward, aged seven, pass sentence of death on her prisoners.

γ. Cruelty of the Yorkists. Execution of Owen Tudor after Mortimer's Cross. General proscription of Lancastrian leaders after Towton 1461.

Many executions by Tiptoft Earl of Worcester, the Constable, who illegally tried his Lancastrian prisoners according to Roman Law.

C. Third Period, **1461–1485**.

(1) The victories of Hedgeley Moor and Hexham, **1464**, established firmly the Yorkist power and made Edward IV less dependent upon the Nevilles, whose support had ensured his succession.

(2) **1471**. The power of the Nevilles was broken at Barnet, Margaret's army was routed at Tewkesbury, and the Lancastrian cause was ruined for a time.

(3) Final Lancastrian triumph at Bosworth **1485**.

III. The Effects of the Wars of the Roses.

A. They led to the end of the baronial supremacy owing to the destruction of the power of the two parties.

The towns and agricultural districts took little part in the war, which was waged by the barons and their retainers. The country generally was not greatly affected. Trade continued and justice was regularly administered during the struggle. Froissart notes that "there are no buildings destroyed or demolished by war, and the mischief of it falls on those who make the war."

B. They led to the establishment of Yorkist and Tudor absolute monarchy, to a period of "constitutional retrogression."

(1) Parliament had been growing gradually stronger since Edward I's time, and the unsuccessful "Lancastrian experiment" was based on the idea of a limited monarchy.

(2) Parliament was rarely summoned by the Yorkist kings, who legislated through the Council, imposed arbitrary taxes (benevolences), and interfered with the liberty of the subject by illegal imprisonment.

(3) The Tudors called Parliament more frequently, but used it as the instrument to carry out their own wishes.

But Parliament continued to exist, and successfully reasserted its supremacy in the seventeenth century.

References :

A. *English Men of Action*, " Warwick," *passim*.

B. Shakespeare, *Henry VI*, Part III :—

> Act I, *Scene* 4 (battle of Wakefield): " Brave warriors, Clifford and Northumberland," and " She wolf of France, but worse than wolves of France."

> Act II, *Scene* 1 (second battle of St. Albans): " Ten days ago I drown'd these news in tears."

C. *Where Avon into Severn Flows*, by Frederick, Lothrop. *In the Wars of the Roses*, by Green, Nelson.

THE KINGMAKER

Richard Neville Earl of Warwick and Salisbury, son of Richard Neville Earl of Salisbury, married Anne Beauchamp, heiress of the Earl of Warwick.

First Period of Opposition to the Crown.

> Opposed Somerset and fought at the first battle of St. Albans, **1455**. Fled to Calais (of which he was Captain) after the defeat at Ludlow. Returned **1460**, seized London, defeated the Lancastrians at Northampton, but neglected to attack the Lancastrians in the North. Strongly resisted York's demand of the crown after the battle of Northampton, but agreed to his ultimate succession after Henry VI's death. Defeated by Margaret at the second battle of St. Albans, **1461**, joined Edward Earl of March at Chipping Norton, and marched with him to London, where Edward was crowned King.

II. Second Period.   The Chief Minister of Edward IV.

A. The war.

> After Towton Edward left to Warwick and Montague the direction of the war. Warwick subdued Wales and overran Northumberland. Montagu finally conquered Northumberland at Hedgeley Moor and Hexham, **1464**.

> After **1464** Warwick's support was no longer essential as Edward's power was firmly established.

Q

B. Foreign policy.

Warwick wanted an alliance with France against Burgundy and urged Edward to marry Bona of Savoy, sister-in-law of Louis XI, and to marry his sister Margaret to a French prince.

(1) **1464**. Edward announced his marriage with Dame Elizabeth Grey, daughter of Lord Rivers (formerly steward to John Duke of Bedford, whose widow, Jacquetta of Luxemburg, he had married), and widow of a Lancastrian knight.

Edward's marriage

α. Was a blow to Warwick's foreign policy;

β. Weakened Warwick's position at home.

Edward deliberately advanced his wife's relatives to form a party to counterbalance Warwick. Lord Rivers, the Queen's father, was made an earl and Treasurer. Her sister Katharine married the Duke of Buckingham.

(2) **1468**. Edward married his sister Margaret to Charles the Bold Duke of Burgundy

α. Without the knowledge of Warwick, who was on an embassy to Louis XI.

β. Valuable commercial connections with Flanders were thus ensured.

Warwick's brother George was dismissed from Chancellorship.

III. Second Period of Opposition to the Crown.

A. Warwick fled to Calais, married his daughter Isabel to Edward's brother, Clarence, and supported his claim to the throne.

Warwick was probably implicated deeply in the rising of Robin of Redesdale,[1] supported by his cousin, Sir Henry Neville. The rising was directed against the Woodvilles. Edward IV was taken prisoner at Edgecote, and Lord Rivers executed, **1469**.

Possibly Sir John Conyers, who had married Warwick's cousin.

B. Warwick returned to England. Edward was captured and imprisoned in Warwick's castle of Middleham in Yorkshire. He was released, put down in 1470 a Lancastrian rising at " Losecoat Field,"[1] and pretended that Warwick was implicated in it (doubtful, as Warwick was not yet in alliance with the Lancastrians). Warwick and Clarence fled to Calais.

C. Louis XI reconciled Warwick to Margaret, and Warwick's daughter, Anne, married Prince Edward.

    Warwick returned to England. Edward fled to Burgundy. Henry VI was restored to the throne. A truce was made with France, and Tiptoft Earl of Worcester, "the great butcher of England," executed. Warwick was now apparently supreme, but

    α. Clarence was dissatisfied owing to the assertion of Prince Edward's claim to succeed before him.

    β. The Lancastrians did not trust Warwick, and Margaret and Prince Edward remained in France.

D. Edward landed at Ravenspur, nominally to regain his ancestral possessions, was joined by Clarence, Warwick was defeated and slain at Barnet, 1471. Margaret was defeated at Tewkesbury, Prince Edward was slain in battle — not murdered afterwards by Richard of Gloucester as is often stated.

    End of opposition to Edward IV.

IV. **Character and Importance of Warwick.**

A. He shows the constitutional position of the leader of the Opposition in the Middle Ages. The risings against Somerset and Edward IV were not purely factious, because at that time armed resistance was often the only means of ensuring a change of policy. Warwick resisted the Yorkist claim to the throne until the policy of Margaret made the assertion of that claim necessary to ensure his own safety.

[1] So called because the conquered Lancastrians threw away their coats to facilitate their flight.

B. Warwick is the most conspicuous example in English history of the " Overmighty Subject."

(1) As Earl of Warwick and Salisbury he had great estates in South Wales, Gloucestershire, Warwick shire, Oxfordshire, Wiltshire, Hampshire, and the North Riding of Yorkshire. His power was greatest in the north, where he held strong castles at Raby, Middleham, and Barnard Castle.

(2) He possessed great military power; he raised very great armies from his own estates and six hundred retainers followed him to Parliament.

(3) He was Captain of Calais and Admiral. 1461 made Steward of the Duchy of Lancaster. Grand Chamberlain, Warden of the Cinque Ports and Scottish Marches.

(4) Supported by the Neville connection.

Brothers
{
John, Lord Montagu, created Earl of Northumberland, 1464.
George appointed Chancellor and Archbishop of York.
}

Uncles
{
Lord Latimer.
„   Fauconberg.
„   Abergavenny.
}

Cousin . John Mowbray, Duke of Norfolk.

5. His riches and power enabled him to act as "Kingmaker." From 1461-1464 he was supreme. Then Edward IV, seeing the danger arising from Warwick's great power, raised up the Woodvilles as rivals to Warwick.

C. He was a great statesman and administrator.

His policy was at first constitutional. Later he met the treachery and ingratitude of Edward IV with diplomacy and intrigue.

D. He was a good general, though possibly lacking in personal bravery, and a most successful admiral.

E. At times cruel, jealous of rivals, but his opposition to
the Woodvilles and his lavish generosity made him
popular, and "he had ever the good voice of the
people."

References:

A. *English Men of Action*, "Warwick," by Oman, pp. 234–43.

C. *The Last of the Barons*, by Lytton, Routledge.

EDWARD IV

I. **After 1471 he was very Powerful.**

A. The death of Prince Edward (in the battle of Tewkesbury)
ruined the Lancastrian cause, which had received severe
blows at Towton, Barnet, Tewkesbury. There was now
no descendant of Henry IV left. Edward IV claimed
the crown unchallenged, by male descent from Edmund
of Langley, son of Edward III, and female through
Lionel of Clarence.

B. The King was rich (unlike the Lancastrians).

α. Benevolences, or forced loans, a new kind of
extortion, yielded large sums.

β. He held the York estates, and confiscated those
of the Lancastrians, especially of the Kingmaker.

γ. Great profit was derived from the law courts
(which did good service in checking disorder).

δ. **1475.** Got from Parliament a generous grant for
war with France, and at Pecquigny from
Louis XI £15,000 and £10,000 a year for not
fighting.

ε. Made much money by trade.

II. The Yorkist Absolutism.

A. Parliament.

Unlike the later Tudors, Edward IV avoided calling Parliament; he was able to "live of his own," and did not need grants.

1475–1483. Parliament met only once, and then made no grants. Summoned in 1483 only because of expected war with Louis XI, who was arranging a marriage of his son to Mary of Burgundy, in spite of the Treaty of Pecquigny, by which he had been betrothed to Elizabeth of York.

Edward IV's reign was a constitutional disappointment. "For the first time since the days of John not a single law which promoted freedom or remedied the abuses of power was even proposed."

B. Justice.

The King interfered with the course of justice. He intervened personally in the trial of Clarence. He sanctioned the use of torture, and prisoners accused of treason were deprived of the right of trial by jury.

C. Administration.

The administration was weak. The nobles retained great power, and frequently oppressed the people.

III. His Foreign Policy.

His indolence prevented him from taking advantage of the opportunities afforded by his kinship with Charles the Bold. But

A. Charles the Bold was fickle, unstable, continually diverted from steady opposition to France by trouble in the Netherlands and by his attempt to extend his dominions to the Rhine.

B. France was more united and Guienne, formerly strongly English, was no longer likely to rebel.

C. Thus the Treaty of Pecquigny was a wise arrangement, but a disgrace to England.

D. Internal troubles in Scotland averted danger from the North. There was no active intervention in Scotland except a successful expedition of Richard of Gloucester, who regained Berwick, 1482.

IV. A Strong Supporter of Trade.

A. Edward IV engaged in trade himself.

B. 1474. He granted the Hanse merchants a settlement in the Steelyard, London, exempt from the authority of the Corporation.

C. Great growth of commerce in his reign.

V. A Patron of Art.

He was interested in Caxton's work, and some of his supporters, especially Tiptoft, "the Butcher," and Earl Rivers (Edward's brother-in-law), were strong supporters of the Renaissance.

VI. His Character.

A. He had shown himself, when necessary, vigorous and energetic.

B. He was a most skilful general, e.g. against Warwick and Margaret, 1471. A clever diplomatist, e.g. in regard to Louis XI, caring little for honour, but gaining great practical advantages.

C. He was cruel to his enemies. He approved of the death of Clarence (probably actually drowned in a butt of Malmsey wine, though possibly poisoned by a cup of that wine) and Henry VI. But he did not oppress the common people.

D. He was very popular owing to his handsome person and affable manners.

E. But after his throne was secure his character deteriorated. Relying absolutely on his brother, Richard of Gloucester, "he rusted away in inglorious ease and self-indulgence,"

F. He was one of the worst men who have sat on the throne of England, and his premature death was due to his evil living.

References :

A. Stubbs' *Constitutional History*, Vol. III, pp. 199–226.

B. *Short History of the English People*, p. 292.

C. *White Wyvill and Red Ruthven*, by Green, Nister.

RICHARD III

Son of Richard Duke of York, brother of Edward IV. Married the Kingmaker's daughter Anne.

I. Before 1483.

He had shown himself a bold and successful soldier in the Wars of the Roses and Scotch expedition 1482, supporting the Duke of Albany against his brother, King James III. A good administrator, especially in North Yorkshire and Durham, where he had received the Kingmaker's lands, and was very popular.

He was absolutely faithful to Edward IV, who left the government largely to him.

He probably fell owing to overweening ambition when the opportunity of securing the throne unexpectedly occurred. In prosecuting this object he showed himself ruthless, cruel, and treacherous.

II. The Claim to the Throne, 1483.

A. He relied upon his northern followers, who occupied London. He was helped by the Duke of Buckingham (created Constable) and Mowbray (given the Duchy of Norfolk).

B. He arrested and (on day of his accession) executed Earl Rivers and Lord Richard Grey, Queen Elizabeth's brother and son by her first husband.

Thus broke the power of the Woodvilles.

C. He got possession of Edward V and his brother the Duke of York.

Hastings, a faithful friend of Edward IV, was summarily executed, because likely to oppose the deposition of Edward V.

D. His chaplain, Dr. Shaw, in a sermon at St. Paul's Cross, asserted the illegitimacy of Edward IV's children, owing to his betrothal before he married Dame Elizabeth Grey, and because he had been married "in a profane place contrary to the law of God's Church." He even said that Edward IV himself was illegitimate. The son of Clarence was declared ineligible owing to his father's attainder. Richard was accepted as King by a few citizens at the Guildhall owing to the presence of Buckingham, and by Parliament owing to a display of force.

Richard crowned King.

Up to this time there was no national resistance. Richard was personally popular and the Woodvilles were hated.

III. The Murder of the Princes.

Possibly owing to a plot against Richard made by the Marquis of Dorset (Edward V's half-brother) the two princes, Edward V and his brother Richard of York, were murdered by Richard's orders.

The popular suspicion of Richard's guilt was correct, and confirmed by the discovery of bones during repairs to the White Tower 1674.

This, the most brutal murder of the times, was a blunder as well as a crime, and was the main cause of Richard's fall. It led to the revolt of Buckingham, who made terms with Morton (Henry of Richmond's agent). A rising in the south and in Wales failed owing to a flood on the Severn which prevented Buckingham from joining the southern rebels, and owing to a storm which scattered Richmond's fleet.

IV. Richard's attempt to strengthen his Position.

A. Execution of Buckingham, 1483.

B. Many excellent laws passed by Parliament, 1484.

1. The jury system was improved.

2. Serfs on the royal estates were enfranchised.

3. The navy was reorganised.

4. A postal service was formed.

5. Customs duties were lowered (books to pay no duty).

6. Benevolences were declared illegal.

C. Treaty with Brittany, where Richmond had taken refuge. But Richmond fled to France, where the Regent strongly supported him.

D. Treaty with Scotland.

E. Richard III obtained the support of the Pope by promising the obedience of England.

V. His Fall.

A. No one could trust him and the Lancastrians, the Woodville party and the friends of Buckingham were united through fear.

B. Although his wife Anne Neville was alive, he proposed to marry his niece Elizabeth of York, and thus alienated many.

C. In spite of the statute of 1484 he extorted benevolences in 1485 and this caused very grave discontent.

D. He lost nerve owing to remorse for the murder of his nephews. "Whenever he went abroad his body was privily fenced and his hand ever on his dagger."

E. His supporters deserted him.

   1. The Stanleys let Richmond (who had landed at Milford Haven) pass Shrewsbury unmolested.

   2. Northumberland refused to go into action at Bosworth.

   3. Stanley deserted on the field.

     Richard fought with the utmost bravery and "died like a king" at Bosworth, 1485.

References :

A. Stubbs' *Constitutional History*, Vol. III, pp. 226–340.

B. Shakespeare, *Richard III :*—
    ACT I, *Scene* 1 : " Now is the winter of our discontent."

C. *The Black Arrow*, by Stevenson, Cassell.

THE SAXON CONQUEST OF HAMPSHIRE

The account given on page 9 has been generally accepted and is supported by Dr. Hodgkin. But the theory that the Jutes were the original conquerors and that the Saxons entered Hampshire from the north about A.D. 600 deserves consideration.

A. The Jutes.

   1. Even in Roman times the Jutes had made small settlements on the mainland, especially in lonely places along the river Meon. After the Romans left larger Jutish settlements were made in the Meon valley and possibly to the west of Southampton Water.

2. The ornaments, arms and utensils found in **1900** in a burial place at Droxford on the Meon strongly resemble those found in Kent which was undoubtedly colonised by the Jutes.

B. The Saxons.

1. No Saxon weapons have been found in Hampshire.

2. The Saxons steadily made their way westward along the Thames, and about 571 made settlements near Oxford and near Wallingford.

3. The first West Saxon bishopric was planted at Dorchester (near Oxford), and not at Winchester, which is not mentioned in the Chronicle until 643.

4. It is possible that the Thames valley between Oxford and Reading, and not Hampshire, must be regarded as the beginning of Wessex.

Compare *Political History of England*, Vol. I, pp. 90–3 with *A School History of Hampshire*, Clarendon Press, pp. 36–9 and *England before the Norman Conquest*, Oman, pp. 225–6.

INDEX TO PART I

INDEX TO PART I

iii

INDEX TO PART I

INDEX TO PART I

Elementary Latin Translation.
By HILLARD and BOTTING. 2s. 9d.

Graduated Latin Selections.
By HILLARD and BOTTING. 4s.

Elementary Latin Exercises.
By HILLARD and BOTTING. 3s. 6d.

Latin Prose Composition for Middle Forms. By NORTH and HILLARD. 4s. 6d.

Additional Latin Exercises.
By HILLARD and BOTTING. 3s.

Latin Unseens.
Junior Course, 2s. 6d. Senior Course, 3s. By HILLARD and BOTTING.

Passages for Translation.
(150 Latin and 150 Greek.) 4s. The Latin separately, 2s. 6d. By HILLARD and BOTTING.

Latin Test Papers. Elementary, Junior and Senior. By A. R. FLORIAN. 1s. each.

Initia Latina.
By E. D. MANSFIELD. 2s. 6d.

Exercises in Latin Prose.
By E. D. MANSFIELD. 3s. 6d.

Porta Latina. A First Latin Trans-lation and Exercise Book. By A. R. FLORIAN. 2s. 6d.

Junior Latin Prose Composition.
By H. J. DAKERS. 4s. 6d.

Continuous Latin Prose Composi-tion. By H. J. DAKERS. 5s. 6d.

First Latin Translation Book.
By A. H. THOMAS. 2s. 6d.

Latin Lessons for Beginners.
By A. R. S. HALLIDIE. 2s.

First and Second Latin Lessons.
By C. M. DIX. 3s. 6d. each.

First and Second Latin Books.
By C. A. WILLIAMS. 3s 6d. each.

Rivington's Class Books of Latin
Unseens. (a) 5 Books for Middle Forms, and (b) 2 Books for Upper Forms. 9d. each.
Easy Latin Unseens. In Three Books. Prose and Verse together :—
Book I. 9d.; Book II. 9d.
Book III., Verse only. 9d.

Single Term Latin Readers.
1st Term. One Book. 10d.
2nd Term. Three Books. 1s. 3d. each.
3rd Term. Two Books. 1s. 3d. each.
4th and 5th Terms. Four Books. 1s. 6d. each.
6th Term. One Book. 1s.

Elementary Greek Translation
Book. By HILLARD and BOTTING. 4s.

A Primer of Greek Grammar.
By E. ABBOTT and E. D. MANSFIELD. 4s. or separately:—Accidence. 3s.

A Primer of Greek Exercises.
By W. GREENSTOCK. 4s.

Elementary Greek Exercises.
By HILLARD and BOTTING. 3s. 6d.

Greek Prose Composition.
By NORTH and HILLARD. 4s. 6d.

Greek Unseens.
Junior, 2s. 6d. Senior, 3s.
By HILLARD and BOTTING.

Greek Test Papers.
Junior, 1s. 3d. Senior, 1s. 6d.
By A. R. FLORIAN.

A First Greek Reading Book.
By ARTHUR SIDGWICK. 3s.

Stories from Herodotus, in Easy Attic Greek. By J. S. PHILLPOTTS and G. C. ARMSTRONG. 3s. 6d.

By W. G. Borchardt.

Elementary Arithmetic. 3s.
Part I, separately, 2s.

Practical Arithmetic for Schools.
5s. 6d. ; or in Two Parts, 3s. each.
Examples only, in Two Parts, 2s. 6d. ea.

Junior Practical Arithmetic. 2s. 6d.
Examples only, 2s.

Arithmetical Types and Examples.
5s. Examples only, 3s. 6d.

Junior Arithmetic. 2s. 6d.
Examples only, 2s.

Revision Papers in Arithmetic. 2s.6d.

Arithmetic Test Papers.
Junior and Senior, 1s. 3d. each.

A First Course in Algebra. 3s.

A Second Course in Algebra. 4s.
The First and Second Course in 1 Vol. 6s.

Elementary Algebra. 5s. 6d.
Or Part I. 3s. 6d. Part II. 3s.
Examples only, 3s. 6d. ; Parts, 2s. 6d. ea.

Revision Papers in Algebra. 2s. 6d.

Junior Algebra. 3s. 6d.
Examples only, 3s.

Algebra Test Papers. Junior and Senior. 1s. 3d. each.

Geometry Test Papers. 1s. 3d.

School Statics and Dynamics.
7s. 6d. each.